SURFING
A Beginner's Manual

www.fernhurstbooks.co.uk

SURFING
A Beginner's Manual

Wayne 'Alf' Alderson

fernhurst
BOOKS

Copyright © Fernhurst Books 1996

First published 1996 by Fernhurst Books,
Duke's Path, High Street, Arundel, West Sussex,
BN18 9AJ, UK. Tel: 01903 882277.

British Library Cataloguing in Publication Data:
A catalogue record for this book is available
from the British Library

ISBN 1 898660 24 7

Acknowledgments
Wayne Alderson would like to thank the
following for their help and assistance in putting
this book together:
Gul Wetsuits, John-Paul Etock, Tiv Thomas,
Nick Sime and Ma Sime's Surf Hut at St David's,
Mike Rogers, Twr-y-Felin Outdoor Centre
at St David's.

Photographs
Photographs by Wayne Alderson and
Alex Williams, plus Gul Wetsuits (shots of
boards and wetsuits), Rick Abbott and
Tiv Thomas. Cover photo of Todd Presage,
courtesy of Gul.

Edited by Tim Davison & Jeremy Evans

Cover design by Simon Balley

DTP by Creative Byte

Printed in China
through World Print

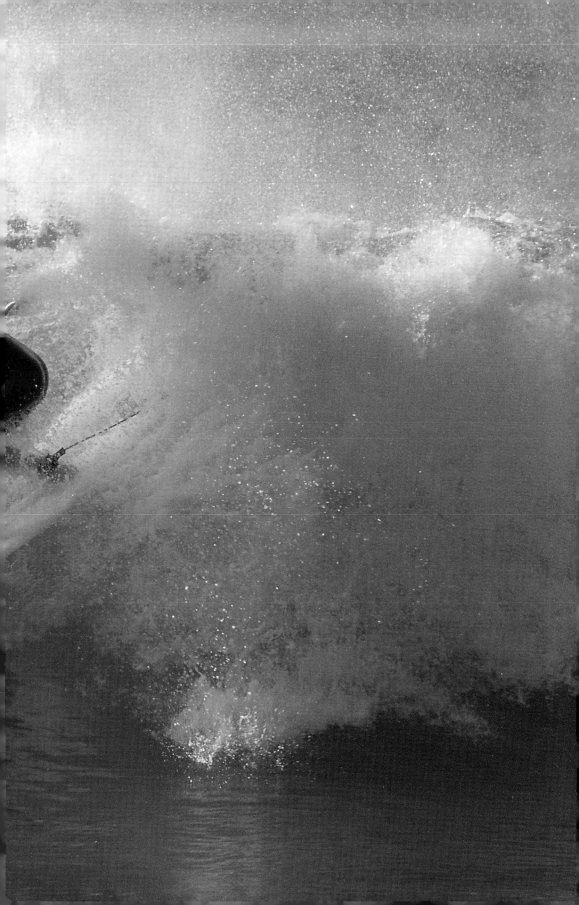

Contents

Prologue

You are about to embark on one of the most difficult sports. However, in return for the difficulties you have to overcome, the rewards are immense. Words can't describe the sheer joy of riding a big, clean wall of water, tucking as the lip folds over you, and looking out on the world from inside a swirling green cylinder of ocean. As the advert says, 'Only a surfer knows the feeling', and this book should help you experience that feeling.

Whatever your level of ability you can get a kick out of the power of the ocean, be it as a learner on a three foot beach break, or as an expert on a 20 foot reef break. But beware, once surf fever strikes, you're stuck with it - possibly for life. Ride one good wave and you will want another one, a better one - and it is that constant search for a better wave that will help you improve - and make you into a better surfer.

Happy surfing! Is there any other sort?

Russ Winter
(in action below)

Foreword

This book is aimed at anyone getting into surfing. Since the early 1980's surfing has grown almost exponentially, and thanks to improvements in wetsuit technology there are few coastlines in the world that have not had their waves ridden – even Alaska, Scotland and Norway now boast their own surfers.

In the book we look at the basics of surfing. You will not find details of how to pull aerials or ride 15 foot reef breaks. By the time you are ready for that, you won't be needing an instruction book! What you will find is all you need to get up and ride your first wave. If the surf conditions are right, you are a reasonably fit and competent swimmer and you are determined enough, you should be able to achieve this within two to three days. You may not be ripping the waves apart, but you should be on your feet with a modicum of control over the board. From there on it is up to you. I have known people who changed their entire lifestyle to improve their surfing, but there are a few pointers on how to get better which include more than just "Buy a ticket to Hawaii".

Whatever your aspirations, there can be few sports that get you hooked the way surfing does. It doesn't matter if you become a contest hotshot or a mellow soul who wants to cruise along a gentle beach break – once you are riding waves you are sure to have as much fun as anyone can with their clothes on.

Wayne 'Alf' Alderson

1 Equipment

The majority of surfers are still riding shortboards, despite the resurgence of longboards in the 80's and the introduction of funboards in the 90's.

Choosing the right gear is essential if you want to make good progress as a beginner, but it is not just a case of walking into your friendly local surf shop and sauntering out again 15 minutes later ready to rip.

Surfboard design is an art form in itself, and no two surfers will ride the same board in the same way or get the same out of it. This is not the place to go into detail on the intricacies of board design (see Chapter 7), but we can take a look at the most popular boards on the water.

SHORTBOARDS

The majority of shortboards will be three fin 'thrusters', usually within the size range 5ft 8in/1.70m to 6ft 8in/2.0m. Bigger surfers may go for slightly longer boards; longer shortboards (excuse the oxymoron) are used in bigger surf.

Shortboards are for more experienced surfers, being highly manoeuvrable, but are at the same time more difficult to control. Various features of the board will be designed to suit a surfer's riding style. Thickness and width vary from board to board, as do rocker and vee. Rails may be hard or soft, the board may have channels, the fin configuration can differ, and tail shape will also vary. (If all this is as clear as mud, see Chapter 7 to understand the terminology.) As you can see there is a lot more to a surfboard than meets the eye, and a lot of time and money is spent on board design and development.

You should forget about getting a high performance shortboard if you are just starting out – after all, would you buy a Ferrari if you

A funboard is a modern compromise that spans the gap between longboards and shortboards.

A typical modern longboard, descended from the old Malibu style which started it all.

The mini-mal is shorter and relatively wider than the standard longboard.

were just learning to drive? It may look cool on the beach, but it will do you no favours in the surf. You will find it difficult to paddle, difficult to catch waves with, and difficult to ride. What you should be looking for is a funboard or longboard.

FUNBOARDS

A relatively recent development in surfing, funboards are mid-way between a shortboard and a longboard. They will usually be around 7ft 6in/2.30m in length, and be slightly wider and thicker than a shortboard, with a more rounded nose. These boards are basically designed for having fun on, as the name implies. They make it easy to catch waves, but can be almost as manoeuvrable as a shortboard. Funboards are ideal if you surf in an area where the waves are generally small or lacking in power. They are also good for beginners.

LONGBOARDS

Longboards are the boards that are associated with the halcyon days of the 60's, when everyone who was anyone 'rode the nose' at every opportunity and drop-knee turns were the only turns worth doing. They were superseded in the late 60's and early 70's by shortboards, but made a come-back some 15 years later, and now most breaks will have a number of longboards out in the line-up.

A longboard will generally be over 8ft 6in/2.60m in length, with a much more rounded nose than the previous two categories, and a wider and thicker template. They may have three fins or one. Also falling loosely within this category are **mini-mals**, which are basically 'short' longboards of between 7ft 6in/2.30m and 8ft 6in/2.60m in length. A smaller longboard or mini-mal can be useful to learn on, as they offer a lot of flotation and stability and are easier to paddle. However, in big surf they can be bulky for beginners to handle.

A pop-out may lack the style of a custom board, but is usually easy to sell on to another beginner when you move up to something more challenging.

Safety first! A soft skin may not look cool, but it hurts less when you get hit.

Longboards are the least manoeuvrable of the three main categories, and are ridden in a different way. The style is generally much smoother and more graceful than that of the shortboarder, with an emphasis on 'walking the board' (moving up and down on the deck of the board) and nose riding (surfing with five or ten toes over the nose - 'hang five' and 'hang ten' respectively). Having said that, high performance longboard surfing, featuring shortboard-style moves, is becoming increasingly common on today's lighter, performance-oriented longboards.

POP-OUTS

A pop-out can be any of the above designs built in a mould, whereas a custom board is shaped and finished by hand. A pop-out can be an excellent first board for a number of reasons. For a start a new pop-out will be about a third of the price of a new custom board, as well as being much sturdier and far less prone to damage. Pop-outs do not have quite the same smooth flowing lines as custom boards, being thicker and wider and somewhat more rough and ready due to the moulding process, but at this stage that is exactly what you want.

SOFT SKINNED BOARDS

In many ways these are the ideal boards for beginners. Generally around 7ft 6in/2.30m in length, they are light, buoyant and stable, and best of all do not hurt too much if they hit you – being made of soft polyurethane foam like the dreaded boogie board. This can be a real confidence-booster for a first-time surfer, who is already being knocked this way and that by the waves without having the additional worry of being hit by an unwieldy lump of fibreglass.

CHOOSING YOUR BOARD

Get a board that will help you to improve rather than one that simply looks good! A pop-out is the best option but if you really want to go for a custom board, a funboard or a mini-mal would be best. What you are looking for at this stage is flotation and stability in the board, which will make the difficult task of balancing on it that much easier. Ideally you should look for something between 12in/30cm and 18in/45cm longer than you are tall. Most boards these days have three fins, although you do occasionally get single or twin fin boards, and sometimes boards with four.

You will find that prices vary from area to area, so shop around. A good surf shop should be able to advise you on what sort of board is most appropriate for your skills. It is best if you can also take along a friend who surfs to give you some advice. Unless you have plenty of cash, it is also well worth considering a second-hand board as at this stage you do not know if you are going to like surfing (although if you don't you should seek medical advice as it's quite possible you're dead). A good second-hand board can be picked up for around half the price of a new one, and some surf shops may even let you give it a trial run which is never the case with a new one.

Be careful with second-hand boards though. They have all had their fair share of knocks, and if the foam is starting to discolour in too many places (where it's let in water through a damaged surface) it is usually best to leave it. Check for soft spots where the fibreglass is delaminating from the foam. This is usually the result of compression from the weight of the surfer's feet. You should also make sure there are no cracks around the base of the fins where they join the board.

The shortie is ideal for warm summer conditions when there's no more than a slight chill.

WETSUITS

A wetsuit keeps you warm by trapping a thin layer of water close to your body, which is then warmed by your body heat. This is flushed out when you wipe-out so the suit needs to be a tight fit - and you need to wipe-out as little as possible!

The kind of wetsuit you need will obviously depend where you surf, and can vary from a 5/3mm full steamer for cold climates (5mm body and 3mm arms), to nothing more than a vest or spring suit for warm areas. Developments in wetsuit and neoprene technology in recent years have resulted in design standards,

Summer steamer or winter steamer? Thicker neoprene panels and full length arms set them apart. (Photos courtesy of Gul.)

warmth and comfort that were unthinkable 15 years ago, and with a good wetsuit you should never feel the cold too badly in all but the most miserable climates.

Fit is everything with a wetsuit though. Advice from a surf shop and/or experienced friends should be sought, but trying a suit on and stretching and bending in it is the only way to be sure it is going to fit. Do not be afraid if you start looking like something out of a kung-fu film, particularly when trying on a full suit - you will end up in far stranger positions once you get into the surf, and you need to be very sure the wetsuit will stretch with you.

After you have used your wetsuit, always rinse it in fresh water. This will extend its life and also stop it from smelling!

The wetsuit should not be too tight, but should fit snugly everywhere on your body with the possible exception of your shoulders where you need a bit of room for paddling. If there are any folds of neoprene it's too big; if you are having trouble breathing and the blood supply to your wrists and ankles is feeling restricted, it's too small.

The extras which make it possible to rip the
waves include a surf leash, a nose guard and
surf wax or deck grip.

Full wetsuits come in a wide variety of styles, particularly with regard to the zip - front zip, shoulder zip, back zip. The effectiveness of each is open to debate, so just go for the style you feel most comfortable in. You will also find different stitching techniques, different types of neoprene, and different thicknesses. The best way around this confusion is to ask the advice of friends or the surf shop staff in the area where you intend to surf – they will know what is most appropriate for the different seasons.

Many experienced surfers have different wetsuits for winter and summer, and maybe one for spring and autumn as well. As a beginner you do not want to fork out on a whole wardrobe of neoprene, so go for whatever will allow you to get in the water most often in most comfort.

You can find second-hand suits, but look carefully for holes, rips, tears and patches. Once a wetsuit starts to go there is not much you can do to stop it, and most repair jobs do little more than delay the inevitable. They can also make the suit more uncomfortable to wear.

SURF TIPS

☆ *Go for function not fashion with your first board - you'll be riding waves sooner.*

☆ *Don't be afraid to ask for advice from surfie friends and in surf shops.*

☆ *Make sure your wetsuit is a good fit – even if it costs. Otherwise you won't enjoy yourself in the surf and learning will be slower.*

☆ *Get a rash vest, especially for use with a second-hand wetsuit.*

☆ *Watch for the sun – even in cold climates you can burn.*

☆ *Protect your ears if you surf in cool waters.*

Rash vests

A rash vest is an invaluable and relatively cheap accessory – a close fitting Lycra vest worn under a wetsuit which stops the wetsuit seams from rubbing. In the days before they were 'invented', several consecutive days of surfing would often lead to a surfer having horrendous wetsuit rubs around the shoulders and armpits, especially with a poorly-fitting suit. Rash vests are also useful as protection from the sun when surfing in warmer wetsuit-free zones.

Additional neoprene

Depending on where you surf and your tolerance to cold you may also need to buy wetsuit boots, gloves or mitts, and a helmet. In cold climates these can be a necessity rather than a luxury. Wetsuit boots are also useful to avoid spiked feet on reefs and in waters where sea urchins lurk. These should be a good fit or they end up like water-filled balloons around your feet. Fingerless neoprene mitts are also popular with some surfers - they theoretically improve your paddling power, although they weigh your hands down slightly. In addition they can provide quite good insulation in cold water.

EXTRAS

Leashes

The leash attaches to your ankle (above whichever foot is to the rear of the board), and basically stops you from losing the board after a wipe-out. Most leashes are made of urethane, with a velcro ankle strap. They attach to the 'deck plug' on the board. Make sure you have a bomb-proof knot, and that the leash does not pass across the rail of the board when at full stretch, otherwise it can cut through the board. Most leashes come with a 'railsaver' to prevent this.

While leashes are obviously of great value, preventing long unwanted swims and loose boards from hurtling towards shore, they should be used carefully. Make sure the leash is the recommended length for your board and the size of waves you will be riding, and after a wipe-out cover your head/face with your hands on surfacing. The leash can bring the board skimming back across the water to you, and the first thing that surfaces will be the first thing it hits - your head. It does not happen often, but it is no fun when it does. I have the scars to prove it!

Leashes also tangle around things such as rocks, your feet and small dogs, so always take up the slack when carrying your board. Most people wrap their leash around the fins and tail.

Nose guards

This is a rubber guard for the nose of your board, one of the most accident-prone areas. It will also prevent you from being speared by the board. An over-priced but useful accessory.

Wax/Deck grip

One undervalued aspect of wax is that it supplies the classic introduction for lone surfers at a strange break - "Got any wax, mate?". It is simple stuff, easily forgotten, but you cannot surf without it on your board. Made from a mixture of paraffin and beeswax, it comes in different hardnesses for different water temperatures. If you surf without a wetsuit you will find the wax can rub and cause a rash on your chest, stomach and the inside of your legs. A combination of rash vest and calamine lotion can reduce the discomfort. Most waxes have some sort of exotic smell such as coconut to evoke memories of warmer waters for those of us far removed from

The largest wave in the world occurs every day on every beach in the form of the tide. It has a wave-length of half the circumference of the Earth, travels at 700-800 miles an hour, and 'breaks' once every 12 hours and 25 minutes.

swaying palms, and they also come in a variety of colours. The brand names are usually designed to shock your grandmother. A useful accessory if you use wax is a wax comb. This allows you to roughen up the surface of old wax on your board, which can tend to lose its 'grippiness' after a while. Eventually you will need to remove the wax and put on a fresh coat.

Alternatively, you can use deck grip, a rubber patch that sticks to the board and gives a good grippy surface for your feet. It also provides some protection against delamination of the deck resulting from the weight of the rider. Make sure your deck is totally clean before application otherwise it won't stick. A lot more expensive than wax but it only needs applying once.

Sun protection

Everyone should be aware of the importance of protecting their skin from the sun, especially surfers who are probably more prone to sunburn than most. Wear a high factor waterproof sun cream or even total blockout, especially if you have fair skin, and re-apply frequently. This is doubly important in warmer climates, but even in colder areas you can easily suffer sunburn if you are in the water for a long time in summer. In addition, rash vests are a good way of protecting your upper body from the sun without getting too hot.

Ear protection

Anyone who surfs on a regular basis in cold water should seriously consider wearing ear plugs in the water. The reason? Cold water and cold winds can have the effect, over a long period of time, of causing a bony growth in the ear canal. This is the body's attempt to protect the inner ear from cold, and eventually it can

A board about to snuggle up in the protection of its very own board bag.

lead to water becoming trapped in the ear and even partial deafness. It can be treated, but this involves painful surgery and the growth can recur. Most surf shops in cold climates should stock ear plugs. Blu-Tack is a cheap but effective alternative. It may not look very sexy having plugged-up ears, but it's worth it - I should know as I suffer from surfer's ear myself (pardon?).

Board protection

Custom surfboards are fragile and expensive, so it is worthwhile investing in a board bag to protect your investment. There is a huge range available for all sizes of board, and some will take two or more. As with all things, the more you pay the better the product you get.

Head protection

Another relatively recent development has been in lightweight surf helmets - almost exclusively made by Gath. Personally I like to keep the gear I wear in the water to a minimum, but I can see that helmets have their uses in big, gnarly reef surf. Even in a smaller beach break I suppose one could be an advantage if it saved a fin going through your head and turning your brain to jelly.

2 First Steps

GETTING FIT

You've got your equipment, now to use it. But hold on, not so fast - there are a few things you can do before hitting the surf that will make the learning experience more rewarding and effective.

The first is to get as fit as you can. Surfing requires strength, speed, stamina and agility, and anything you can do to improve these will be well worthwhile. You don't need to end up looking like Arnie Schwarzenegger, but you should think specifically about developing your arms, shoulders, upper back and neck, and improving your cardiovascular fitness and overall agility. Of course the best form of exercise and the most enjoyable is surfing itself, but getting in trim before you start and then keeping in trim will make things that much easier.

Swimming

We will assume you can swim to start with. In fact you should be able to swim AT LEAST 50 METRES IN OPEN WATER to ensure your own safety if you get into difficulty. So, why not start off with a visit to your local pool, or better still the sea (in your new wetsuit - good way to get a feel for it) and swim some more. It is a good way of increasing your fitness, and many of the muscles you use are the same as those used in surfing, especially if you do the crawl.

Home exercises

There is not the space here to go into specific exercise routines. Any library will have books that can help, or you could join a gym and get a tailor-made training programme.

Balance sports

Associated 'balance' sports can also help a great deal. Snowboarding and skateboarding are more or less land and snow-based versions of surfing, with similar manoeuvres and very similar balance techniques involved, and for cold-climate surfers snowboarding makes an excellent winter alternative. However, snow skiing doesn't give much benefit. Although good for balance and general fitness, turning on a pair of skis makes you move your body in exactly the opposite way to surfing, which can be confusing when you transfer from one sport to the other.

Skateboarding is one of the closest land-based sports to surfing. You may not need to swim, but the falls can come harder.

SURF SCHOOLS

While this book aims to teach you the basics of surfing, you really cannot beat direct tuition on the beach or out in the surf. Try to get at least one lesson from a qualified surfing instructor, as it undoubtedly speeds up the learning process and makes you more safety-conscious. There are surf schools on most coastlines that are popular with surfers. You can get addresses and phone numbers from the relevant surfing association (see chapter 10 for details).

SHORE SURFING

If you have access to a swimming pool in which you can take your board, why not use it to practice paddling? OK, it doesn't look too cool, but this is one of the most strenuous aspects of learning to surf, and the more you can practice it the better. For more details on paddling technique see the next chapter.

Another useful exercise on dry land is getting to your feet on your board. But make sure you do it on a soft surface, otherwise you could easily damage your board before you get it in the water, especially if it's a custom job.

To do this, first of all lie on your board. Assuming that you have a good beginner's board of around 7ft 6in/2.30m in length, you should have your feet about 6 inches/15cms from the back of the board when you are lying on it. This will obviously depend on how tall you are, but basically there should be about 10-12 inches/30cms of the nose of the board lifted off the water surface when you are paddling it if your weight is distributed evenly on the deck. As the board is not on the water you cannot really judge that, but you can usually sense what feels right.

Put both hands flat on the deck directly under your shoulders and push up as if you were doing a push-up.Take your body weight on your arms and hands. Once your upper body is off the board, bring your forward leg up under your chin, at the same time twisting your hips so your backside faces out to one side.

Your rear foot should follow so that you are now in a crouching position with your feet about shoulder width apart down the centreline of the board. Quickly stand up straight, with both feet flat on the board and still the same width apart, and your arms out to your sides for balance. Both feet should have the stringer running under the middle of them, and be at approximately 90 degrees to the stringer along the centreline of the board.

This whole movement should take about a second to perform in one fluid motion. Do not worry if it is a bit stilted at first, as it will come in time. Watch experienced surfers taking off on a wave and you hardly even notice them get to their feet - they seem to be suddenly standing and riding.

Do not try introducing a 'halfway' stage of kneeling on the board before getting to your feet. Once you are on a wave this will make getting to your feet both slower and more difficult, and is a very bad habit to get into - you will never see an experienced surfer do this.

Practising like this is of course no substitute for the real thing, so now let's hit the beach.

1. Paddling for the wave. Note the position on the board – not too far forward, not too far back.

2. Slide the hands back, ready to push up on the board.

3. Hands flat on the deck, ra̶ upper body off board.

It is not a bad idea to carry the board with the fins forward and the leash wrapped tightly around the tail.

ON THE BEACH

Carrying your stick

Before getting to the basics of wave riding, there are a few simple points worth considering. First, carrying the board. Now this may seem the kind of thing any fool can do, but some fools get it wrong. Do not, for example, drag your board behind you - it won't do the board any good, and just looks slack. Also, don't let the leash drag behind you. Once again it's bad for the equipment, and you or someone else may trip over it. Think about which way round you carry your board. I say this because I used to carry mine with the nose forward and the deck facing out, until one day I took a slice out of my heel when I caught it on a fin while running down the beach. Since then I carry the board fins-forward.

Waxing-up

To read some surf mags you could be forgiven for thinking there is an art to applying

ouching position, sliding correct stance.

5. Front knee beneath chin, body angled in direction of travel, feet comfortably apart – a well-balanced stance.

6. Riding position – arms out for balance, look where you are going, not down at your feet!

wax. All that is involved is common sense. You may want to apply a base coat which helps the top coat adhere, but with either coat give the board a good covering. Rub the block over the board lengthwise then crosswise or in a circular motion, until you get small bumps of wax appearing on the deck.

Apply a fresh layer every time you surf until it starts to get too lumpy and dirty (it should be fairly obvious when this stage is reached), at which point it can be scraped off with a hard, smooth edge (such as a credit card) after being left to melt in the sun.

Make sure you get the right wax for the water you're surfing in. Warm water wax will be difficult to get on in cold conditions, and in warm conditions cold water wax will just smear across the deck and refuse to stick. In hot weather it is a good idea to cool the deck of your board in the sea before waxing up – it will go on more easily. Finally, don't rest your board on a hard or uneven surface when you wax it – the pressure you apply could ding the underside.

Smell that coconut! What could be more exotic than a block of surf wax?

INTO THE SURF

Those cool green cylinders peeling into the beach may look inviting, especially as you see another surfer cruising along, but there is a lot of work involved in getting out to them!

First of all, check the waves. Sit on the beach for a few minutes watching the waves break. Are they too big? Check the size against other surfers in the water. Is it too crowded? More chance of collisions, especially for beginners. Are there any obvious rips and currents? These can be very dangerous in the wrong hands. Is the wave suitable? You want a gentle, rolling break rather than a heavy, pounding one. Make sure you are comfortable with all these factors before going out into the surf - if you are nervous in the water you will not perform to the best of your ability.

Once you get to the water's edge attach your leash. Clean any sand and gunge out of the velcro on the ankle strap, and ensure the cord itself is on the outside of your ankle. If it is on the inside there is more chance of getting snagged up on it. Now wade out in the water with your board nose-first under your arm, lifting it over approaching waves, until you are about knee-deep. At this point float the board beside you with the nose pointing out to sea, again lifting it over oncoming waves. Never place it in front of

Checking out the surf is always a very good idea before you dash in, especially at an unfamiliar break.

Ensure you put your leash on properly – you don't want it coming off in the surf.

Entering the water, board tucked comfortably under your arm.

you - an oncoming wave can easily push it straight into you.

Keep one or both hands on the deck to control the board as you are pushing it out. You can also rest your weight on the board if you are walking across an uneven or rocky sea bed to help you balance and/or to stop the rocks from cutting into your feet. If a wave catches you by surprise, try to hold onto your board. The easy option may be to let it go, safe in the knowledge that it is attached by the leash, but there may be someone behind you for it to bounce off first. So

if you really *have* to let it go, check there is no-one behind you first. (See 'Safe Surfing' in Chapter 5.)

Research indicates that 10 per cent of all waves are over 20 feet/6 metres in height, and 25 per cent are between 3-4 feet/1.0–1.20 metres.

Approaching an oncoming wave – make sure the board is at your side to avoid its being pushed back into you.

Lift the board over the wave as it passes you, then continue to wade out with the board by your side.

'BELLYBOARDING'

Once you get into waist to chest-deep water, turn the board shorewards when you get a lull in the surf. To start off with you are going to 'prone in' to the beach as if you were riding a bellyboard - this will give you a feel for the board and the surf.

To do this, wait until a broken wave approaches you, and when it is about two metres away push off the bottom with your feet and lie on your board, all the time holding a rail in each hand. Try to get into the position we discussed earlier – not too far forward or too far back. Too far forward and the board will 'pearl' which means the nose will dive under the water and you will be thrown over the front; too far back and you will have difficulty picking up the wave.

As the wave picks you up, slide your weight back a little to avoid nose-diving (or 'pearling'), then once your are moving slide forward again. If you lean one way or the other you will find the board will turn in the same direction - try this to get some idea how the board reacts to shifts in body weight.

After you have done this a few times, you should start paddling for the approaching wave rather than just hoping it will pick you up of its own accord. Lie on the board looking over your shoulder at the approaching wave. Start to paddle for it when it is about four metres away, using alternate strokes. When you feel the wave pick you up, paddle one or two more strokes to ensure you have caught it, then lift your arms out of the water, grip the rails and ride into the beach. Adjust your weight back and forwards on the board as necessary to stop it nose-diving or stalling.

The wave has picked up the surfer, who grips the rails for balance and makes slight adjustments of body weight to allow the board to trim, retaining maximum planing speed. Note how he keeps his head well up so he can see what's coming.

Stopping the board

You may need to get off the board before the wave has faded under you, especially if you are on a collision course with someone else. To do this, either slide off the side of the board holding firmly onto the rails, or move to the back causing the tail to dig in and stall the board.

Traversing the wave

The next step is to bellyboard across the face of the wave rather than straight into the beach. Paddle for the wave as above, and once you have caught it lean left or right until the board turns. Don't be too brutal about this or you will probably fall off. If you do it gently you will feel the board start to turn, and as long as you keep the weight lightly angled on that side of the board you will find yourself traversing along the wave. If you maintain too much weight on the rail the board may turn over the top of the wave. By shifting your weight around you will be able to make the board do shallow 'S' turns along the wave as you ride towards shore.

Once you are catching waves easily and bellyboarding with confidence, you're ready to have a go at standing up.

The surfer looks behind to see the approaching wave while paddling for it. After the wave has picked him up he grabs the rails and shifts his weight to allow the board to plane. Once the wave has broken he moves his weight slightly forward to compensate for the lessening speed of the wave. Note how he is also traversing across the face of the broken wave rather than riding straight forward.

Paddling for the wave, the surfer feels the wave pick up the board, arches his back and tucks his arms beneath him prior to pushing up. From there he moves quickly into the crouching stance, then puts out his arms at the same time as bending his legs for better balance. Note how he looks shoreward all the time, and adjusts arm position and stance to adapt to the changing charac-teristics of the wave.

STANDING UP

So this is it, the hardest thing you will come across in learning to surf. Once you have mastered this the rest will follow sooner or later if you stick at it.

Walk out with your board to the same point where you were bellyboarding and in a lull between sets turn the board shorewards, then lie on it. Keep checking behind you for the next set. Give about four hard strokes on each side, and when the approaching wave picks you up give a couple more. Then go through the motions you practised on the beach as quickly as possible:

1. Push up with your arms, hands flat on the deck. Arch your back as the wave picks up the back of the board to keep the nose from pearling.

2. Slide your legs up so your leading leg/foot is just beneath your chin, and your rear foot about shoulders' width behind. Your front foot should be at a slight angle to the central stringer, the rear foot between 45 and 90 degrees to it.

3. From this crouched position get to your feet as quickly as you can, holding out your arms for balance and keeping your knees bent. By shifting your weight between your front and back foot you will be able to lift up the nose of the board or push it down, which slows it down or speeds it up respectively.

4. Let the board take you in a straight line toward the beach.

Kneeling is OK when you're first starting out and getting a feel for balancing on the board, but try to avoid getting into the habit – it makes it much harder to get to a standing position.

This all sounds like a hell of a lot to remember while you are struggling with an unfamiliar object in an unfamiliar medium, but understanding the technique involved is half the battle - if you know what you are supposed to be doing before you start, it will make the whole thing come naturally that much more quickly.

At first you will find it difficult, if not impossible, to get from lying down to standing up in one quick, smooth movement. Don't worry about this. You may find it easier to learn the whole thing in stages - prone, kneeling, crouching then standing. If this is easier for you, go for it. However, try to avoid getting into the habit of kneeling as it's more difficult to get to your feet quickly from a kneeling position. Good style, in the long run, is about a quick and fluid movement from lying to standing. Stick at it, you will get there eventually!

If you're going to wipe-out why not be flamboyant? Seriously, note how the surfer is already covering his head for protection as he heads towards the foam. This is not always possible in a high speed wipe-out, but you should still remember to protect your head with your arms and hands when you're surfacing.

WIPE-OUT!

No one said this was going to be easy, and one thing you will do a lot is wipe-out. Even this has a technique to it. When you feel you are losing your balance, try to fall away from the board and land in the water as flat as you can. This lessens the chances of you being hit by the board, and of bouncing off the bottom – hard-packed sand can feel as solid as concrete if you hit it with too much force.

In small waves wiping-out can be a laugh – in bigger waves it can be serious. Even in small waves though, especially when you are learning and probably nose-diving, the board may be flung into the air after you wipe-out and can easily land on you. Always cover your head with your hands and arms for protection, and do not surface immediately - count to three first, so the board has time to land.

In bigger surf you should try to fall away from the impact zone as well as away from the board to ensure you do not get held under too long. Try to go into a ball and roll with the wave, especially if you are surfing a reef break (not that you should be at this stage) as it will lessen the chances of hitting the bottom. If you get held under, try not to panic. Try to get a good fill of air before you hit the water, and open your eyes once under so you can swim to the surface avoiding turbulent patches of water. Once you are on the surface, check straight away to see whether another wave is about to break on you - at least you can be prepared for another hold-down.

When you surface after a wipeout, remember that your board is attached to you by a leash. Although it rarely happens with modern equipment, the leash can occasionally act like a rubber band and bring the board winging back across the water towards your head. You will soon get some idea of whether this is likely from the amount of pull on your leg. If the board is pulling hard on the leash it probably means it is at full stretch and may come back quite quickly once the pressure eases.

Whatever the situation, it is always best to surface with your hands and arms shielding your head to ensure you do not end up with a fin through the skull. Above all, try not to panic. Most waves will rarely hold you under for more than four or five seconds.

Board recovery after a wipe-out

If you wipe-out in water that is too deep to stand in, you need to scramble back onto your board without the assistance of a 'foot-up'. To do this get yourself midway along one side of the board, grab each rail, and submerge the back end of the board so you can 'float' onto it. Then simply adjust your position - you may have to slide forward a bit - and paddle back out.

Even the best fall off. Pro surfers in France demonstrate one of the universal truths of surfing – everybody wipes out sometime.

Turning right (above) and turning left (opposite), both on broken waves. Note that right/left refer to the turn from the surfer's point of view and not as viewed from the beach.

LEFT, RIGHT, LEFT

Once you feel confident about riding the board in a straight line towards the beach you can start learning basic manoeuvres. To be honest, turning a surfboard in white water does not have a lot in common with pulling turns on an unbroken wave. The main aim here it to become more confident standing on the board, and develop a better feel for what this length of fibreglass is capable of doing under your command.

So, once you have caught a broken wave and are on your feet heading towards the beach, have a go at turning left or right. The board will only turn to a limited degree, as the white water on either side will tend to push it back shorewards, so try the turns when you have as much speed as possible – that means as soon as you get to your feet when the momentum of the board will act against the white water.

Turning a surfboard is all about weight placement, and most of the weight is invariably placed on your rear foot/leg. Assuming you are a 'natural' foot surfer – you surf with your left foot forward – and you want to turn right on the wave, you should put your weight on your right (or rear) leg whilst leaning your upper body right, arching your back slightly and holding your arms out to your side to aid balance. If you want to turn left, again put your weight on your

back foot, but this time weight your upper body to the left and very slightly backwards. For goofy-footers who surf with the right foot forward the process is simply reversed.

Turning the board so that you face the wave as you're riding is surfing 'forehand'. Turning so that you have your back to the wave is surfing 'backhand'. Most surfers – even experienced ones – find it easier to surf forehand, so do not worry if you feel a little uncomfortable on your backhand.

This may all sounds straightforward enough in black and white, but remembering it when you are out in the surf is another matter. Keep at it though, and you will win in the end.

ANGLED TAKE-OFFS

Angled take-offs allow you to start traversing the wave immediately you get to your feet. As a beginner this avoids the difficulty of pulling a bottom turn. For more experienced surfers it allows them to beat sections of breaking or broken water, or to stay ahead of the lip of a fast breaking wave. On a broken wave, have the board angled very slightly left or right as you take off – not too great an angle though, or the wave will probably lift the side of the board and push you off.

The more quickly you can get to your feet the more effective an angled take off is in traversing the wave, and the fact that you have taken off at an angle should enable you to ride the wave diagonally towards the beach.

Taking-off at an angle sets you up in the right direction to ride across the wave.

HELPFUL HINTS

Learning to get to your feet is the hardest part of learning to surf, and can be the most demoralising if you are making slow progress. You can help yourself by:

1. Getting as fit as possible before you start learning.

2. Persevering – if it does not come straightaway, do not give up. We all have different learning abilities and rates of uptake. Just because you are slower than your friends at getting to your feet does not mean that you will not be as good or even better once you have learnt to stand up – seriously!

3. Being motivated. If you really WANT to learn to surf, you will achieve your aim.

COMMON MISTAKES

The old saying 'you learn from your mistakes' is very true. Here are the most common ones amongst beginners. If you know what they are you will know how to avoid them:

1. Kneeling before standing up.

2. Weight too far forward on the board can lead to pearling, or weight too far back can make it difficult to catch waves.

3. Getting to your feet in stages – it should be one quick, fluid movement.

4. Trying to stand up before the wave has been caught properly.

5. Too stiff and upright once on your feet – *bend ze knees* and maintain flexibility.

6. Feet too close together.

7. Feet/body not at correct angle.

8. Not shifting body weight to vary speed and/or turn the board.

 **SURF TIPS**

⭐ Don't push the board ahead of you when wading out – a wave could easily push it back into you.

⭐ If you surf with your left foot forward you're a 'natural' foot surfer. Right foot forward and you're a 'goofy'. These are ancient terms – don't let anyone tell you they're taken from those upstart snowboarders!

⭐ Watch where you're landing when you wipe-out. Try to avoid hitting anyone else with your board.

⭐ After a wipe-out always surface with your hands and arms protecting your head.

⭐ The golden rule of wipe-outs, especially bad ones, is try not to panic. It's very rare to be held under for longer than you can hold your breath – unless you're out in bigger waves.

 The largest breaking wave ever recorded was around 112 feet/34 metres high.

3 Into the Surf

Once you have got the hang of riding the white water straight into the beach you will want to get out where the real waves are. You do not want to be looking for anything very big just yet, and a wave with a three foot face is quite adequate at this stage.

In order to ride unbroken waves you are going to have to paddle out through the surf. This will mean fighting your way through lines of white water, learning to paddle efficiently, and learning how to sit on your board - no more pushing off from the sea bed now!

Paddling out in nice easy relaxed style, well positioned on the board.

PADDLING OUT

This is the most strenuous part of surfing. Anything you can do to build up your arms, shoulders and back and make them more supple will be well rewarded at this stage, but you can still be pretty sure you are going to be as stiff as a board (ha! ha!) after your first few sessions – stick with it, you will soon tone up.

If you get a flat day while you are on the coast, why not just go out and paddle your board? It is good exercise for when the next swell arrives, and you even get to see the beach from a different angle - but don't go too far out unless you are a competent swimmer and are sure of local rips and currents *(see Chapter 6 for more details)*.

Having pushed your board out until the water is about waist deep, you should be ready to lie on it and start paddling. Walking out any deeper is just hard work, and paddling is quicker and more efficient. Make sure you are in the right position on the board first. You should have a feel for the board by now, and it should be fairly obvious if you haven't got it right – too far back and the nose will be high out of the water and the board will paddle slowly due to drag, too far forward and the nose will dive making the board difficult to paddle. If you are not sure you are doing it right, compare the way your board is lying in the water to other surfers around you.

Once paddling you should use smooth, alternate strokes of the arms, like doing the crawl. Keep your hands slightly 'cupped', with each hand and forearm entering the water smoothly and sweeping low across the water surface. Too high is wasting your energy; too much splashing is a sign of poor style. Try to apply equal paddling force with each stroke - if one arm strokes more powerfully than the other you will find yourself moving out to sea at an angle, although this is obviously the way to turn the board when you wish to do so.

At the same time as you are paddling you should have your back arched and your head raised so you can see what is happening in front of you – particularly useful if a big set comes through! Don't arch your back too much as it will

WAVE SIZE

Estimating wave size is a vague science at best - a three foot wave in Hawaii would be six feet or more in most other places, as waves are measured from behind in 'the islands'. In effect this gives the size of the swell rather than the wave face which is likely to be twice as great. Elsewhere there is often a 'macho' element to the sport that underestimates wave size - it is supposedly cool to call a wave that is quite obviously overhead "three to four feet". For the purposes of this book we will assume a three foot wave is around waist high on the average adult, and a six footer is about head high.

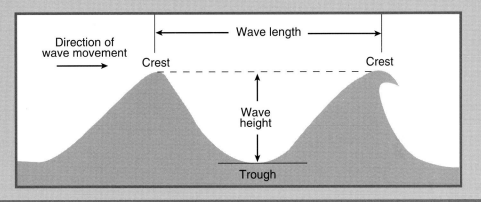

cause excessive strain. You will still find this position puts a lot of strain on your neck, shoulders and lower back, and it is a good idea to stretch the various muscles associated with these parts of the body before you enter the surf. Exercising them on a regular basis is a good idea: swimming is ideal.

It also makes very good sense to do a warm-up routine before entering the water, stretching the arms, shoulders, back and neck in particular. Find a sequence of exercises that allows you to do this on the beach before you paddle out – ok, it may look a bit pretentious, but if it is good enough for the pros (check them out stretching before their heat in a contest) it has got to be good enough for you. The reason is quite simple. Loosen up the muscles that will be doing most work and they are less likely to seize up on you. If you strain a muscle out on the water it will be uncomfortable at best and agonizing at worst, and it could put you out of the water for days if not weeks, particularly if it is in your back. It is also not much fun trying to get back in through the surf with a bad back.

What we have covered so far in terms of paddling assumes you have been out in flat water, which is the last thing you want if you are learning to surf. In the real world you will initially be paddling out through small waves, but even then can sometimes get 'caught inside' by a bigger set or a 'sneaker' wave (a wave that is bigger than everything else that has been coming through). This can be quite worrying when you consider that research has shown that one wave in a thousand (maybe one every four hours) can be twice the average size. From my own experience it would seem to be less frequent than this, but there are occasions when a three foot swell will suddenly be invaded by a six footer. This is why larger waves are not recommended for beginners - imagine being out in five foot surf when that one in a thousand wave arrives!

GETTING THROUGH A BROKEN WAVE

Discarding the board

As a beginner, your first instinct when caught inside will probably be to chuck your board and dive deep to avoid being pummelled by white water. That is fine at the early stages AS LONG AS THERE IS NO-ONE BEHIND YOU. If you are going to discard your board always check first that you are not putting anyone else at risk. If there is a chance your board may hit someone, do all you can to keep hold of it.

Assuming it is safe to discard your board, you can either dive head first beneath the oncoming wave, or slide off the side of your board and, using it as a platform, push up on it, then sink feet first below the wave. This is usually all you need to do in smaller surf. As with a wipe-out, don't forget to protect your head from flying surfboards when you surface.

My final advice is try to move away from discarding your board in the face of an oncoming wave as quickly as you can. That is safer for everyone.

Holding onto the board

If you decide to try holding on to your board, slide off the side as the wave approaches and hold tight with both hands towards the front of the board, pushing the nose underwater just before the wave hits you. The wave will push you back somewhat, but you will not lose time retrieving the board.

In smaller waves you can also move forward on the board as a wave approaches, and push the nose under the water just before the white water hits you. Lie flat on the board holding the rails, and let the white water wash over you. Once it has done so, slide back and continue paddling. A couple of paddling strokes just before the wave hits will give a bit of momentum to get through it.

Another option in small waves is simply to push up with your arms and lift your upper body from the board, so that the white water passes between you and your board. Or, if you are sitting on your board while out in small surf you

The surfer lies flat on the board and allows this small wave to roll over him, comfortably making it through the wave.

This surfer pushes himself up from the board to allow the wave to pass between his body and the surfboard, then sinks back down onto the board and continues paddling out.

can 'get through' a breaking wave by turning your back to the white water, remaining sitting and leaning back into the wave while gripping the board with hands and legs; then turn back round to face out to sea once the wave has passed. At this stage you may find this technique a little awkward.

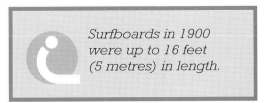

Surfboards in 1900 were up to 16 feet (5 metres) in length.

Leaning back on the board. The resistance of the surfer's body weight and the board prevent a small wave from pushing him back into the beach.

An eskimo roll. As the wave approaches the surfer rolls the board, clinging hard to it from underneath while the wave passes over them. After the wave passes he resurfaces and gets back onto the board to continue paddling out.

Eskimo roll

An eskimo roll requires areasonably good feel for your board and is not something you will be able to do straight away. However with bigger boards such as mini-mals and longboards this may be the only way of getting through larger waves while keeping hold of your board.

You need to hold the rails tight, wrap your legs around the board (although some surfers

A duck dive as a surfer heads out for unbroken waves. (The photos give the view from the beach, the drawings the underwater perspective.) As the wave approaches, the surfer pushes the front of the board down to duck beneath the wave. As the wave rolls over him he transfers

do not bother with this), and roll upside down as the wave approaches, holding tight onto the board. If you keep the board flat in the water the wave should roll over the top of it and leave you more or less where you started from. Remember to keep a tight hold, otherwise the wave can easily rip the board out of your hands. Once the wave has passed over you, flip the board back over, clamber back on, and continue paddling out.

Duck dive

This is a technique used by experienced surfers, and you should not feel under any pressure to be performing them at this early stage. However, it is worth knowing about so that when you are more confident in the surf you can start having a go. It is the most efficient way of getting out through the surf, and skilled surfers will use this technique in double-

his weight to the back of the board using his knee. This forces the nose up and it pops out of the back of the wave. Done properly, he can continue paddling out with very little loss of momentum.

Sitting on the board – looks nice and easy, doesn't it? But even this requires practice.

overhead waves.

As the wave approaches, push up on your board and use your weight to push the front of the board under the water, either just at the

 A wave approaches the beach at 15-20 miles per hour.

A wave will break in water roughly 1.3 times the height of the wave face.

base of a breaking wave or just in front of a broken wave. Once the front of the board has submerged and the wave is passing over you, push the tail down with one knee. The pressure on the back of the board should be enough to push the nose up, so that as the wave passes you surface through the back of the wave and simply carry on paddling.

This is not an easy manoeuvre. It requires practice, timing and a cool head, but as soon as you feel confident enough to give it a go, do so - the sooner you start the sooner you will master it.

Sitting on the board

Once you have fought your way out past the white water you will probably feel like a well-earned rest before you try to catch a wave. Sitting on your board in the line-up is a good way of getting your breath back. However, as with paddling this is not as easy as it may seem. You will almost certainly fall off at first, but don't worry - it happens to everyone else, and they are liars if they say otherwise.

All you can do is practice finding a position on the board in which you feel most stable - usually with the front of the board out of the water and the back end submerged. The angle will vary depending on the length of the board. You can turn the board while sitting on it by using your legs as paddles. Remember to help yourself by making sure the deck has a good coating of wax before you hit the surf.

SURF TIPS

☆ *Paddling out will be hard work at first – but nothing worth doing ever came for free, and riding waves is no exception.*

☆ *Always do warm-up exercises before you go out into the surf – loosen up so you can hang loose!*

☆ *Try not to discard your board when faced by an oncoming wave – always try to hold on to it which is safer and more efficient.*

☆ *Never paddle out directly behind another surfer – if he loses his board after being hit by a wave guess who it's going to hit?*

4 Surf Manoeuvres

Once you have become competent at catching and riding broken waves you will soon want to ride the unbroken face – this is 'real' surfing. A number of basic manoeuvres are described in some detail in this chapter. Once you can do all of these you can with some justification call yourself a competent surfer. More advanced manoeuvres are described briefly at the end of the chapter. As this book is aimed at beginners, there is little point in going into great detail about manoeuvres that you are unlikely to be pulling off until well beyond the beginner stage - but more of that later.

Although you may be tempted to go 'out the back' and try these moves after a few minor successes at standing up on broken waves, try to resist that temptation. Surfing an unbroken wave is a different kettle of fish, requiring a good feel for your board and a reasonable level of confidence in the surf. Half a dozen rides to the beach on white water will not give you either of these attributes, and even if you make it out to the line-up you are likely to become a hazard to yourself and others. Take time to learn the elementary stages, and you will benefit far more when you are ready to head out the back.

THE TAKE-OFF

This is the point at which the whole ride begins, so you need to get it right - otherwise it

A forehand angled take-off. The surfer is already sighting 'down the line' as he gets to his feet, with the board travelling diagonally to the wave face. Note how he pushes down on the front of the board to force it down the face.

Inside out

The inside rail refers to the edge of the board nearest the wave face. The outside rail is the edge furthest from the wave face – and usually nearest the shore.

could end up being a very short ride! There are two methods of taking off:

Angled take-off

As the name implies, this involves taking off at an angle to the wave. It saves having to do a bottom turn (see below) which makes it easier for many beginners.

As the wave approaches, paddle at a slight angle to the shore and the face of the wave. As the wave picks up the board, you will find it is already starting to progress along the face of the

wave. At this stage you should try and get to your feet. This will be more tricky than on the broken waves you were surfing previously. You need to do it more quickly so the white water of the broken wave does not have time to catch up with you, and you also need to have better balance to compensate for the fact that the board is moving at an angle rather than straight forward. Once on your feet adopt a slightly crouching stance with arms apart for balance, and sight along the face of the wave. You will need to shift your weight from foot to foot to get the board into trim, which basically means to get it onto the fastest part of the wave. This is all easier than it sounds and is done very much through feel and experience, so the more often you do it the more natural it will become.

This description assumes you have gone for a forehand take-off. Most surfers favour riding waves forehand as it is generally regarded as easier, mainly because you can see the wave face and what the wave is doing close to the curl. However, some beginners seem to find backhand waves easier to start with. If you are going for a backhand angled take-off, it is pretty

A backhand angled take-off. This take-off has allowed the surfer to just stay ahead of the white water of this crumbling wave.

much the same as doing it forehand although you need to take off at an angle which is a little tighter to the wave. Trimming is more difficult as you cannot see the wave so readily on your backhand, and there can be a tendency to stall.

Don't let this put you off surfing on your backhand. You will need to learn to do so eventually if you are to become a good all-round surfer, and it can be very satisfying to ride a 'harder' backhand wave well.

A forehand bottom turn. Paddling for the wave the surfer uses his weight on the front of the board to increase momentum, gets quickly to his feet, then pushes down hard on the inside rail and goes into a perfect bottom turn. Note the way his 'body' stores the energy of the drop down the face; the front foot 'guides' the board round; and he constantly looks ahead to where he intends to go next.

A backhand bottom turn. The surfer drops straight down the face of the wave, body poised for the release of energy at the bottom ready to turn the board back up the face. Note the use of the arms for balance at the point of turning.

THE BOTTOM TURN

Forehand bottom turn

Paddle for the wave. As it picks you up get to your feet as quickly as you can, then ride the board straight down the face of the wave. At the bottom of the wave push down on the inside rail, gradually increasing the pressure on your back foot so the tail is digging into the wave at the same time as the inside rail. Use your front foot to guide the board round until you are either heading back up to the lip or have straightened out ready to trim along the face. Your body should move smoothly so that at the bottom of the wave your legs are bent, storing energy like a spring which is then released smoothly but quickly to direct the board along the arc of the turn. If you try to throw your body and board into the turn you will more than likely fall off.

Backhand bottom turn

This is more difficult than a forehand turn

A forehand cutback. World champion Kelly Slater demonstrates at the top-level. Note how timing and weight placement are vital with this move.

Many people also find it harder to lean into a turn on their backhand than their forehand. Despite this, the manoeuvre is essentially the same as a forehand bottom turn. Take off straight down the wave, bend your knees and lean into the turn with your weight on the tail and inside rail and guide the board round ready for your next move. You should have your feet almost parallel for this move, and your body weight needs to be angled back towards the face of the wave.

Two things to remember. If you put too much weight on your inside rail and/or tail the board may stall, making it difficult to regain enough speed to stay on the green face of the wave - or you may even wipe out. If you put too little weight on the inside rail and/or tail the board will not respond enough to get you round the arc of your turn before the lip lands on top of you.

THE CUTBACK

Once you have mastered these manoeuvres you will eventually need to learn how to do a cutback. This is used to get you back towards the pocket of the wave, where the power centre is, from out on the face where power is diminished. It is a difficult manoeuvre which involves the essentials of forehand and backhand turns. Until you have them mastered you will have problems with effective cutbacks.

Forehand cutback

Although a cutback is an excellent way to get back to the most powerful part of the wave, timing and positioning are highly important when going for it. If you cutback too soon you may get caught by the white water of the breaking wave; if you do it from too far out on

the face you may not have enough speed and power to get the board all the way round, resulting in a stall.

Once you are out on the face of the wave, take the board as high up the face as you can before transferring your weight to the outside rail. Twist your head and upper body round towards the direction in which you aim to go which is back towards the curl, then put your weight on to your back foot and guide the board round so you are now riding backhand towards the approaching white water. Use your arms for balance throughout the manoeuvre.

Before you hit the white water start to angle the board round to where you have just come from. This means once again putting weight on the outside rail and tail, and weighting your upper body much as if you were doing a forehand bottom turn. Use your back foot to pivot on, turning the tail under this pivot. If you get it right the board will turn as it becomes immersed in white water (or just before), and you will find yourself back in the most powerful part of the wave.

This does not sound easy – in fact at first it is not at all easy for what is supposed to be a basic manoeuvre. The reason is that a cutback is a relatively drawn-out manoeuvre combining two other moves performed quickly one after the other. As a beginner you will probably find it difficult enough performing one manoeuvre at a time, without going for two together. Practice trying gentle turns, and accept that you may get bogged down in white water or stall way out on the face. Once you get it wired, you can make much more of a wave.

A backhand cutback. Notice how adjusting body weight is so important for this move. See how the surfer 'pivots' on his hips as he turns.

A forehand top turn. From a carving bottom turn the surfer heads up the face, placing all his weight on the tail to bring the board around at the lip ready for his next move.

Backhand cutback

In some ways this is easier than a forehand cutback, as once you turn back towards the white water you can see the wave easily – on a forehand cutback it is more difficult to see what the wave is doing. Once again, get as high up the wave as you can. Then place your weight on the outside rail and tail, pivoting round on the tail so the board arcs around to face the white water. Now you can see the face of the wave, but try to keep your head up – there can be a tendency to look down towards the bottom of the wave as you turn the board.

As you approach the white water your weight will be on the inside rail again (this was the outside rail before you turned). Gradually transfer your weight onto the outside rail again, although not so gradually that the white water overwhelms you. As the board turns be careful that the outside rail and the nose do not dig into the water too much – which is a common mistake – before eventually increasing pressure on the tail to swing the board all the way round to set off along the face again. Simple!

THE TOP TURN/OFF THE LIP

You will be pleased to learn that on the whole this is an easier move than a cutback, with the added advantage that it can be practised at the end of a ride as a wave is closing out – so you have nothing to lose if you wipe out when attempting it. The top turn is a re-entry performed just under the lip of the wave; the off the lip is a re-entry performed off the lip as its name implies. There is not a great deal of difference between the two moves except one is slightly higher up the wave than the other. They can both naturally follow a bottom turn as your board heads up towards the top of the wave face.

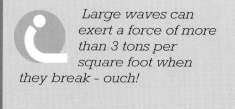

Large waves can exert a force of more than 3 tons per square foot when they break - ouch!

Forehand top turn / off the lip

From the bottom turn, guide your board round and up the face of the wave, looking ahead to judge the point at which you want to hit the lip. As you approach the lip, place your weight hard on the back foot so the fins start to cut into the wave face, while using your front foot to guide the board round. Arms are vital for balance here, but don't flail like a windmill!

You need to make sure the board is well into the arc of the turn by the time you get to your highest point on the face, otherwise you may end up too high on the wave and lose it as it passes beneath you - very frustrating! Once the board is heading back down the face you can decide whether to continue all the way down to shred another bottom turn, or to trim along the face. At first a full-on turn of this type may be more than you can manage. By attempting a scaled-down version, adjusting your weight to move the board up and down the face in elongated 'S' turns, you can approach it gradually.

A backhand off the lip. This is a small wave, but by using all the energy of the wave to maximum effect the surfer is still able to pull off an impressive turn. Note how weight is transferred from rail to rail, and how the arms are used for balance.

Backhand top turn/off the lip

As with most backhand manoeuvres, this is more difficult than the forehand version. Come out of your bottom turn and try to look along the face to the point at which you want to hit the lip. This is harder riding backhand, as you are looking over your shoulder. Push down hard with your back foot, moving weight onto the

inside rail so the board heads back up the wave. At the top of the wave, transfer your weight again to the outside rail, and be aggressive with your rear foot - make those fins cut in!

It's important to use your arms for balance and shift your upper body to help with the weight transfer. The board should by now be heading back down and/or along the wave. Do not keep the weight on the outside rail for too

The end of the line – a kick-out from a closing-out wave.

long, otherwise it may dig in and you will be thrown off the board and down the face of the wave. From here line up your next move.

THE KICK-OUT

All good things come to an end, waves included, but what happens when they do? For most beginners riding a clean wall of water, the last thing to worry about is how to get off the wave after all the time and effort they have spent getting on it. However, you will eventually need to learn how to make a controlled exit. It is safer than just falling off and hoping for the best; it is quicker than falling off as you will be over the back of the wave rather than under it; and it looks more stylish.

A kick-out is really no more than a top turn without the turn. Simply ride the board up the face of the wave, and as you reach the top stall it by putting your weight on the back so the tail sinks into the face. The front of the board should be just over the top of the wave at this stage. As the board stalls, it will inevitably move towards you because it is sinking under you. As it does so, extend your arms, grab the rails, and drop down into a paddling position with the board facing back out to sea. With practice you will be able to land on the deck in exactly the same position as if you were paddling, and thus move from riding to paddling back out in one smooth movement.

WHERE NEXT?

The manoeuvres above make up what many people would consider to be the basics of surfing – which is what this book is all about. By the time you can perform all these with confidence you will be a competent surfer, and this book will have been getting dusty on your bookshelf for some time. So where do you go next? As I said at the start of the chapter, there are no detailed descriptions of advanced surfing manoeuvres here. By the time you are tube riding and performing floaters you won't need a book to tell you what to do. It will be something that comes from the experience and skill you have developed from your own ability and determination. However, it is worth finishing the chapter with a brief description of some more advanced surf techniques so you know what you are seeing down at the beach, and what you can aim for.

Radical manoeuvres such as those which follow require you to surf in the most powerful and critical part of the wave, so you need the experience to read the wave accurately and quickly. You also need a high level of fitness, and the right attitude – you have to really go for it with these moves, and not worry too much about the consequences of not pulling it off, which can sometimes be heavy!

A tube ride. The surfer constantly adjusts his body weight and the trim of the board to stay in the tube.

Tube ride

The classic surf manoeuvre, a good tube ride can live with you forever. Riding inside the lip of a hollow wave, surrounded by moving

Backside off the lip.

Frontside off the lip. Both these advanced moves off the lip require an aggressive and confident technique for success.

water can look deceptively simple and exceptionally cool when performed well, but your timing and positioning have to be spot on otherwise you cannot pull it off. Conditions also need to be ideal - a powerful break with a light offshore wind to hold up the face of the wave and allow it to pitch out and tube. The classic tube is Hawaii's Pipeline.

Weight transfer and trimming is all-important with tube riding – you need to be able to stall your board by putting your weight on the back foot so that the tubing section of the wave can overtake you, but not so much that you get caught by the foam ball at the back of the tube which is essentially the broken wave following up the tubing lip. Once the wave is breaking over you it is necessary to adjust the trim of the board constantly, and also to be ready to shift your weight forward to accelerate out of the barrel. It is possible to get tubed riding frontside or backside, but a backside tube ride is much harder as you can't see what the lip is doing behind you.

Once you have been tubed you will be surfing forever. You will need to catch another... and another... and another...

Advanced off the lip

This is an extension of the standard off the lip described above. All but the tail of the board is brought over the top of the lip, before being brought back round and down the face.

Kelly Slater on the launching pad. Note how he grabs a rail to keep the board in contact with his feet.

Aerial

A potential off the lip can be projected into an aerial by keeping the board going up through the lip and out into air as it breaks free from the face of the wave. The surfer often grabs the rail to keep the board in contact with his feet as it travels through the air, ideally describing an arc before coming down onto the face of the wave, where he continues riding.

Floater

This is used when a wave 'sections' or

breaks in front of you. The board is directed up onto the lip of the breaking wave, then 'floats' across the top of the white water, before eventually coming down with the curtain of water ideally to continue the ride. It can also be used to finish a ride in which the wave is closing out.

The most popular modern board design, the three-fin 'thruster', was developed in the early 80's by Aussie pro surfer and board shaper Simon Anderson.

Kelly Slater again, this time making the most of a close-out by pulling a floater to finish his ride. The need for skilful use of balance and weight distribution is obvious, especially as the board falls with the lip. As with parachuting, landing is the hardest part!

As you can see a 360 is a very difficult move, not least because the white water has time to catch up with you as you're spinning round, making it difficult to get back onto the clean face of the wave.

Advanced cutback

This is as before, but is made with a deeper, carving turn back into the wave, followed by a 'foam bounce' off the white water to get the surfer back onto the clean face of the wave.

Layback

This is a backhand manoeuvre used on steep waves, where the surfer leans back onto the face, using the wave for support. Getting back into an upright position is often the most difficult part of this move.

360

As the name suggests, this is a 360 degree turn which is executed high on the face of the wave. It is difficult, because it takes time to get the board round, and it also involves the surfer remaining in one spot performing the move while the white water may come past and make it difficult to catch up with the clean face of the wave again.

Tail slide

This involves taking the board up the face of the wave, then sliding back down it again tail-

A classic long arc cutback performed on a modern longboard.

first before turning and carrying on along the face. Again, it is a difficult move requiring good balance. Not only are you briefly surfing 'backwards', but the board is also more or less stalled at the base of the wave once it has slipped down the face which makes it difficult to pick up momentum again.

MALIBU MOVES

The traditional malibu boards are ridden 'the same but different' to modern short boards. While good mal riders can pull off most of the moves described above, there are also a few manoeuvres that are generally only practised on Malibus or longboards.

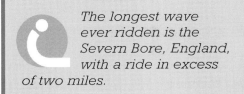

The longest wave ever ridden is the Severn Bore, England, with a ride in excess of two miles.

Drop-knee turn

This involves dropping the rear leg right down on a bottom turn so it more or less touches the deck – hence the name. This was done in the old days as one of the few effective ways of getting a hard turn out of the heavy, unmanoeuvrable longboards of the time.

Walking the board

Again, self-explanatory. In order to get longer boards to trim effectively on the wave it is sometimes necessary to shift your weight about to such an extent that it can only be done by walking up and down the deck. This should be done in a smooth 'foot over foot' action - never shuffle!

A surfer 'walks' towards the front of the board to improve trim – and it also looks good. Wearing a leash makes this move more difficult as there's always the risk of getting the leash caught around your feet.

Hang five/Hang ten

Once you have walked all the way up to the nose of the board, you can further demonstrate your skill by curling the toes of one or both feet over the nose - 'hang five' and `hang ten' respectively. A hang ten in particular is an elegant but difficult move.

Surfing dates back at least as far as the 15th century in Hawaii, and probably much further.

The first westerner to see surfing was Captain James Cook, when he 'discovered' the Sandwich Islands (now Hawaii) in 1771.

SURF TIPS

☆ *Never forget that you need to shift your weight around on the board constantly, even to ride in a straight line – don't stiffen up.*

☆ *Don't thrash around like a headless chicken either – there is no point wiggling your backside around all over the place and waving your arms like a wind turbine if it doesn't achieve anything!*

☆ *Ensure your feet are not too far apart when you stand up. This is a common mistake with beginners, and often results from riding a board that is too short for your ability. This leads to having to have your foot well forward to give the board the necessary momentum to travel along the wave.*

☆ *Practice! Go out even when the surf is border-line – the more time you spend in the waves, the more quickly you'll improve.*

5 Safe Surfing

Once you are out in waves of this size, safety is of paramount importance!

You will find freedom surfing in the ocean. While this is very much a part of the sport, you cannot just paddle out at a break and do exactly what you want in the water. You need to consider both your own health and the health of other surfers and water-users, so this chapter covers the basic common-sense aspects of surfing that are often overlooked by both beginners and experienced surfers alike.

ON THE BEACH

On busier surf beaches you will usually find that the beach and water close to the shore have been 'zoned' and are patrolled by lifeguards. The zoned areas are set aside for various activities, with one or more areas for bathers and surfers. These areas are marked by flags. The generally accepted system throughout the world is that a bathing area will be between flags coloured half red and half yellow, and a surfing area will be between flags with black and white quarters. The surfing area is usually for any form of surf craft, not just surfboards, which can cause plenty of problems (which we will come to later).

An area marked by red flags indicates danger, and neither bathers nor surfers should enter the water. The red flag may actually be flying because a big swell is running and the lifeguards think it unsafe to allow people in the water, but for many surfers these are just the

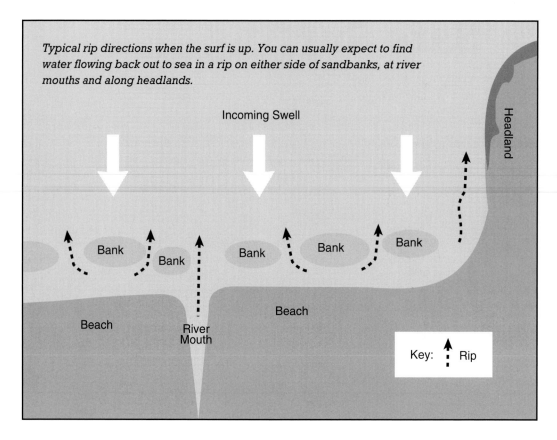

Typical rip directions when the surf is up. You can usually expect to find water flowing back out to sea in a rip on either side of sandbanks, at river mouths and along headlands.

conditions they want! If you choose to ignore the red flags, bear in mind that the lifeguards are under no obligation to assist if you get into difficulties.

In a world brimful of rules and regulations, it may seem too much that even beaches are regulated. However there are sound reasons for zoning. The potential dangers of allowing surfers to ride straight through areas where people are swimming and paddling are obvious – even the most experienced surfer makes mistakes, and in a stretch of sea packed with swimmers the risk of someone getting seriously hurt is plain.

If you are surfing on a beach patrolled by lifeguards, respect their directions. They will usually set aside the part of the beach with the best waves for surfers anyway. If you choose not

to – well, lifeguards seldom come small, and they will be waiting for you when you paddle in, as well as singling you out as the idiot of the day to everyone else on the beach.

RIPS, CURRENTS, TIDES

Rips

Rips are channels of water flowing out to sea. They occur where water pushed up a beach on a swell drains away and back out to sea. It follows that the bigger the swell, the more water is pushed up the beach and the bigger/stronger the rip will be. Rips form either side of the sandbanks on which waves break, at river mouths and along headlands. The water is deeper in a rip and it is less likely that waves will break here - indeed, rips can easily be identified by their lack of waves and by the obvious channel of rippled water flowing out to sea. The rip will eventually weaken and die as it moves into deeper water.

Experienced surfers often take advantage of rips to get out to the surf more quickly, using the flow of water for a free ride. Beginners should treat them with caution though, as once you are in a rip you can easily find yourself drifting out to sea very quickly. If this happens, never panic. All you need to do is paddle at 90 degrees to the rip and eventually you will work your way out of the channel of seaward flowing water. You may now be faced with large walls of white water, however, as you are back in the break zone. This is why it pays to avoid rips unless you know exactly what you are doing. This white water will eventually push you back into the beach, but you could end up with a good drubbing first.

Never try paddling against a rip - unless you are the proverbial Son of King Neptune you cannot beat it. If you are in serious difficulties off a patrolled beach, raise your arm in the air to attract the attention of the lifeguard (the internationally recognised call for help). If the beach is not patrolled, try and attract the attention of other surfers – as an inexperienced surfer the answer is never to go out on your own from unpatrolled beaches.

Currents

Some beaches may have currents flowing horizontally up or down the beach. These may change direction with the turn of the tide (see next section) and increase in strength as the swell gets bigger. Keep an eye open for this phenomenon. At best it may result in your being taken away from the break and having to walk back up the beach to where you started from; at worst you could be swept onto rocks, or in front of a rocky outcrop with the danger of being washed onto it. To ensure you don't get caught unawares by a cross-shore current, take a fix on a landmark on the beach – a house or lifeguard hut for example – and keep checking regularly to make sure you are not drifting too far either side of it.

SELF PRESERVATION

* *Always be aware of your limitations.*

* *Never go out in surf that is too big for you.*

* *Don't stay out too long – once you start feeling tired or cold catch a wave straight back in.*

* *Be aware of the effect of cold water or hot sunshine on your body – both can sap your strength without you necessarily realising what is happening.*

* *Get local advice on possible hazards.*

* *Check your equipment regularly.*

* *Never surf alone, and make sure someone else knows where you are surfing.*

* *Look out for other surfers and water users.*

This small wave is breaking from our right. Both surfers have taken off more or less together. The surfer to our left, furthest from the broken wave, must kick out to give the other priority.

Tides

In some areas tidal ranges can be very large, and there may be a risk of being cut off from your access to the beach as the tide comes in – watch out for this. It is also possible that rips and currents can change strength and direction at different stages of the tide. Local knowledge obviously helps here – you must keep a check on what is going on as the tide ebbs and flows on a strange beach to make sure you never get caught out.

THE 'DROP-IN' RULE

There are few hard and fast rules in surfing, but this is one of them! It applies equally

The surfer on our right is being obstructed by the surfer on the left who has clearly dropped in.

whether you are a grizzled old surf dog or a fresh-faced young grommet. The drop-in rule basically says that on any wave **right of way belongs to the surfer nearest the peak or the white water.** What this means is that if someone else is already riding the wave, you should not go for it.

The reasons are simple. Another surfer taking off on a wave already being ridden risks causing a serious collision. This could injure both surfers or damage their surfboards, and at the very least will spoil the wave for the surfer with right of way who invariably has to take action to avoid colliding with the idiot who has dropped in.

Although all surfers should observe the drop-in rule, beginners must be particularly aware of it. An experienced surfer can usually kick off the wave if he or she inadvertently drops in, but this is rarely so easy for inexperienced surfers. Always look along the wave before you take off to make sure there is no one else riding it or in a position of priority.

Every surfer gets frustrated with this rule at some time or other, because no matter how good you are there are bound to be times when a perfect wave comes through and someone else has priority. C'est la vie, and it will inevitably be worse for beginners, as experienced surfers – especially the locals who know their home break – are constantly able to beat you to the wave. All you can do is grin and bear it, and keep practising so that eventually you become that hot local who is catching all the waves.

BE AWARE

It will by now be obvious (hopefully) that there are a lot more things to look out for when you go out for a surf than simply waves. This is especially so in crowded conditions, which are becoming increasingly common these days, and are the most likely circumstances in which novice surfers will find themselves. With this in mind, here are a few more tips to help you surf safely.

Getting caught inside

This is when a bigger than average set comes through and breaks in front of you – or on top of you. You can reduce the chances of this by keeping an eye on the horizon. If you see what looks like a bigger than average set heading your way, start paddling out to sea so you get beyond the 'impact zone'. It's not a good idea to paddle frantically. You need to keep some energy in reserve in case you do get caught inside – you can then hold your breath as the wave passes over you. So paddle calmly but quickly, and never panic!

We have already discussed how to get through breaking waves (see Chapter 3), but there are bound to be times when you either can't hold your board, don't want to, or simply lose it. If you plan to discard it, make sure no-one else is likely to be hit by it. Just before the white water or the lip hits you, dive as deep as you can, relax, and stay down until you feel the turbulence ease – which will only take a few seconds unless you are out in big surf. Try to

Here the surfer has been caught inside by a rogue set. All he can do is attempt to get through the broken waves by one method or another until the set has passed. It's always possible that this may be the first set of an increasing swell, so it may well be worth sitting further out to wait for the next set in case it's the same size. It will soon become apparent if it was just a one-off.

open your eyes – that way you can see the white water of the wave easing as you swim to the surface. Once back on the surface, beware of your board hitting you as it returns on the leash and look around to see if another wave is about to break on you. If it is, repeat the above. If not, climb back on your board and paddle out past the impact zone.

If you get caught inside badly and are taking a bit of a beating, always remember that as long as your board is attached to your leg, you have your own flotation device. If worst comes to worst, try to cling to it and let the white water push you back to shore.

Canada has the longest coastline in the world at 56,453 miles - it's a shame the surf's so cold.

Surfing in crowds

The surfer riding the wave always has right of way, but this is especially important in crowded conditions. Even if you are paddling out this still applies. Try to paddle to one side of the break, rather than straight through it. This is less likely to cause collisions and is also easier than paddling through breaking or broken waves. The surfer on the wave has right of way, and you should take action to avoid being hit by him or her rather than the other way round - they already have enough to concentrate on in riding the wave. If this means paddling towards the white water rather than over a clean face, so be it.

On the way back in, if you lose control of your board while riding a wave in crowded conditions, try to grab the board so that it travels a minimum distance and doesn't hit anyone. Never wipe out and just hope for the best!

USER-FRIENDLY EQUIPMENT

You can reduce the risk of injury to yourself and others by a few simple measures:

1. Fit a noseguard.

2. Blunt the edges of your fins with sandpaper – it will not change the performance of your board but reduces the chance of laceration if one hits you or anyone else.

3. Check your leash regularly for wear – if it has any nicks or cuts, replace it or it will eventually snap at one of these points. Also ensure that the ankle strap is in good condition, and make sure you fasten it securely every time you go out.

SURF TIPS

 Always remember the drop-in rule.

Be aware of the surfing and bathing areas on patrolled beaches.

Never try paddling against a rip. Always paddle across it, at 90 degrees to it.

Never surf alone on an unpatrolled beach.

When out in the surf keep a constant check on the waves and what other surfers are doing.

Remember your board is an excellent flotation device in an emergency.

 "Whales now number less than seven per cent of what they did at the turn of the century."
Jacques Cousteau

6 Waves & Weather

Someone once asked whether I got bored surfing the same waves at my local break all year round : "Surely it's the same wave every time!". Well, as any surfer could have told him, "No, it's not!". It may look the same to the uninitiated, but every wave is different for a surfer – even those perfect point breaks you see at places like Jeffrey's Bay in South Africa.

But while every wave may be different, it can still be categorised into one of three types - a beach break, a reef break or a point break. The basic features of these are described later in this chapter. However, before moving on it is worth looking at how and why a wave actually breaks.

WAVE FORMATION

As everyone knows, the waves that give us our surf are caused by storms out at sea. The further away the storm, and the more intense the associated depression, the cleaner and bigger the waves that appear on the coastline. As a storm develops, the wind blowing across the ocean surface will first of all cause ripples which develop into chop and then wind waves as the wind strength increases. If the wind continues to blow these wind waves will develop into a 'sea'.

As the waves increase in size the wind transfers more energy as each wave presents a

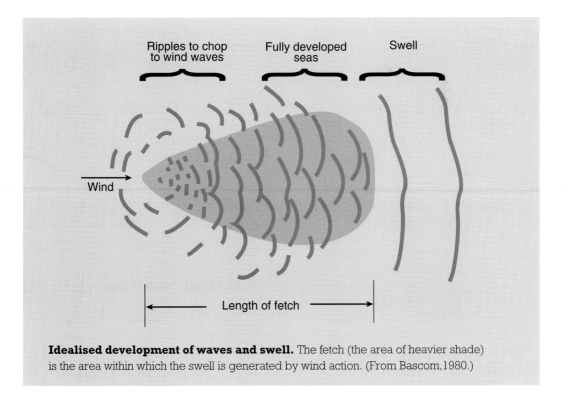

Idealised development of waves and swell. The fetch (the area of heavier shade) is the area within which the swell is generated by wind action. (From Bascom, 1980.)

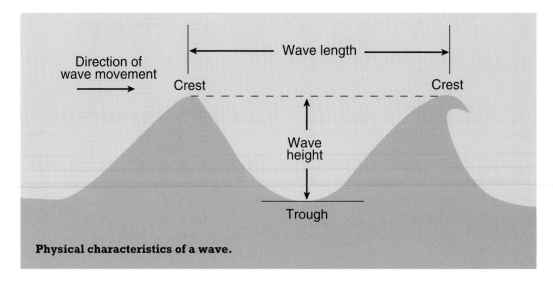

Direction of
wave movement
→

Crest

← ——— Wave length ——— →

Crest

Wave
height

Trough

Physical characteristics of a wave.

larger back for the wind to push against. How large the waves become will depend on the strength (force) of the wind, the length of time (duration) for which it blows, and the amount of open water (fetch) over which it blows. It follows that the larger the body of water over which a wind can blow the bigger the waves are likely to be. This is why you can get huge waves in the Pacific, but never in the Mediterranean.

There is a limit to how much energy the wind can transfer to the ocean, and when this limit is reached the sea is said to be 'fully developed'. It will still be a mass of choppy waves tumbling and spilling over each other, and it is not until the waves move away from the windy storm area that clean, even swell lines can develop, radiating downwind from their source. These swells could then travel up to twice around the globe before dissipating, were it not for the fact that they collide with land masses and breaking waves are formed.

As a swell moves towards a coast (usually at speeds of 15-20 mph) it encounters shallower and shallower water until it starts to 'drag' on the sea floor. This increases the steepness of the wave face, making it less stable until

eventually it becomes totally unstable and breaks. This will normally happen in a water depth of about 1.3 times the height of the wave, so you could expect to find a wave with a 6 foot face breaking in water around 8 feet deep. This may not always be so, especially in the case of reefs which rise abruptly from the sea floor. The energy released when a wave breaks is phenomenal - large waves have been recorded as exerting a force of 6,000lbs per square foot in the impact zone!

Once a wave breaks, it will take one of three forms:

Surging waves

These are waves that come in from relatively deep water to steep beaches, and then surge up the beach rather than break onto it. They are no use for surfing.

Spilling waves

Characteristic of beach breaks, spilling waves are produced by a gently sloping sea bed which causes the wave to peak gradually and thus release energy relatively slowly, so

A surfer on a spilling wave – in this case it's a French beach break.

that the crest 'spills' down the face. Spilling waves are ideal for learning.

Plunging waves

Plunging waves occur when a swell comes in out of deep water, and then hits an abrupt rise in the sea bed such as a rock shelf or coral reef. The wave face will steepen quickly as it 'trips' over the reef, and the lip is thrown out to form a hollow cylinder or tube as the energy of the swell is released very quickly. Plunging waves are favoured by more experienced surfers.

BREAKS

From a surfer's point of view, waves will generally produce a beach, reef or point 'break', depending on the topography of the coastline.

Beach breaks

These are the waves that beginners and less experienced surfers should head for, being generally mellower than reef or point breaks. Beach breaks are at their best on a beach

A plunging wave breaks on a reef on the north shore of Lanzarote.

A good quality beach break.

Neil Harris at Brimms Ness, an excellent reef break in northern Scotland.

Reef breaks

Reef breaks produce the classic hollow tubing wave that all surfers dream of – Hawaii's Pipeline being THE example. These waves are for experienced surfers only, as will become apparent.

A reef break forms where any underwater obstruction rises suddenly above the sea floor - a rock shelf, coral reef, even a submerged wreck. As the swell moves towards the shore from deep water it will come up against the 'reef' which obstructs its forward movement. This will cause the swell to 'jack up' abruptly into a wall of water, throwing the lip of the wave out in front of the face. Under ideal conditions this wall will then peak right or left - or maybe both – to give a fast, heavy wave, usually breaking in relatively shallow water.

where a well defined sandbar has developed – this will cause the swell to peak on the sandbar, and with luck it should peel to left and right either side of the bar.

Beach breaks are fickle creatures which will only last as long as their associated bank. This can easily be destroyed by a storm, so you should not assume that a beach which is renowned for quality waves will always have them. For instance, if the banks have been messed up by storm action the wave could become a 'close-out' (it breaks all at once due to the sea floor being a uniform depth beneath the wave), or it may 'section' (it breaks in more than one place along the face at the same time due to undulating sandbanks). A good beach will have several beach break peaks along its length which may make it possible to avoid crowded conditions. Since beach break peaks can shift as the swell hits them, you don't necessarily have to compete with other surfers huddled around the same spot.

As mentioned, beach breaks are ideal for beginners. You should still bear in mind that the beach breaks on a coastline that picks up powerful swells can still pack a solid punch – this means they can drill you into the sand if you wipe out once the surf gets some size to it. Also, as the surf picks up you must be aware of the progress of rips and currents, as mentioned in the previous chapter.

The speed and power of the wave is a result of the energy of the wave being dispersed quickly over a small area. This gives a great ride, but can also give a heavy wipe-out – and as the wave will be breaking in shallow water over a hard and maybe sharp bottom, a bad wipe-out on a reef break can have serious consequences for both surfer and board. Also, reef breaks generally break in the same spot every time, which means that in crowded conditions competition to get on the peak can be intense. The moral, therefore, is get plenty of experience under your belt before you tackle a reef break.

Bull sharks are so tenacious they have been known to pursue their victims onto land!

A small but perfect point break.

Point breaks

A good point break will develop where a swell hits a coastal promontory or headland and 'wraps' around this natural projection, often with almost machine-like regularity – check out a good video of Malibu in California to see what I mean. As with any swell, waves will form once the swell hits the shallower water inside the headland. This may occur as a result of the deposition of sand from rips and currents running down the headland, and/or from the build-up on the sea floor of rocks and boulders that originated on the headland.

Point breaks provide some of the longest surfable waves, and may run for hundreds of metres down a headland and into a bay. Point breaks can also be quite mellow, and on smaller days sand-bottom point breaks may be OK for inexperienced surfers. However, watch out for the rip that often runs alongside the

The world's most poisonous fish is the scorpion fish of the Indian and Pacific oceans. A sting from the spines on its back can cause death within hours.

SURF TIPS

Start off surfing beach breaks – they are easier to learn on and less painful to wipe-out on.

Learn to read a weather chart for the area where you surf, and work on 'local' knowledge if you want to catch more waves.

Be sure to check the weather forecast every day, so you know when surf is on the way.

associated headland. This will get stronger as the swell increases. As with reef breaks, point breaks generally break around the same spot on any particular swell, which can lead to fierce competition to catch a wave.

CATCHING THE WIND

The man in the street is usually of the opinion that good surf requires a howling onshore wind to blow in some 'great rollers'. The surfer in the water knows he couldn't be more mistaken. Ideal surf occurs when a good swell coincides with a gentle offshore breeze, which helps to hold up the face of the wave, makes it more hollow and causes it to 'peel' cleanly. As this book is being written by the less than balmy waters of the British coast, I'll look briefly at the way in which the ability to read a weather chart for the North Atlantic can increase your chances of scoring good waves. If you live beside a different sea or ocean, the principle remains the same.

And it's simply this:

What you should look for on a weather chart is a deep depression out in the ocean, while the landmass on which you live is under a nice calm high pressure system.

The depression will be creating a swell which will then emanate from the 'epicentre' and arrive on the coast a day or two later, or maybe more, depending on how far it has to travel – once you get to know local weather patterns well, you can usually predict how long a swell will take to reach your beach to within a

few hours. The longer the depression remains offshore the longer the swell will pump through, and as long as the high pressure remains overhead you should get calm conditions, or offshore or maybe cross-shore winds. Then, as the depression approaches land the wind will start to go onshore and mess up the associated swell. If you surf on an indented stretch of coastline or a peninsula you may have breaks that are offshore while others are onshore, so local knowledge can be vital in making the most of a given swell.

This is only a basic description of how weather patterns affect surf characteristics. If you want to know more, there are plenty of books at your local library all the way up to PhD level!

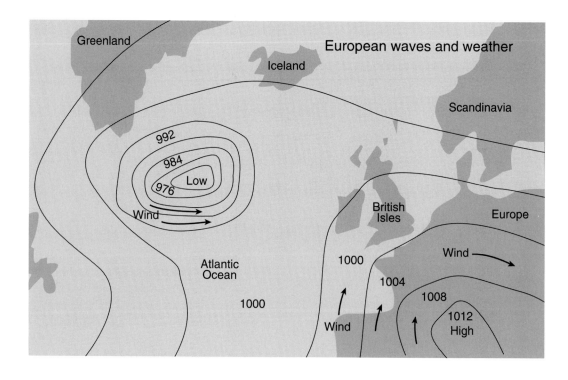

7 Surfboard Design

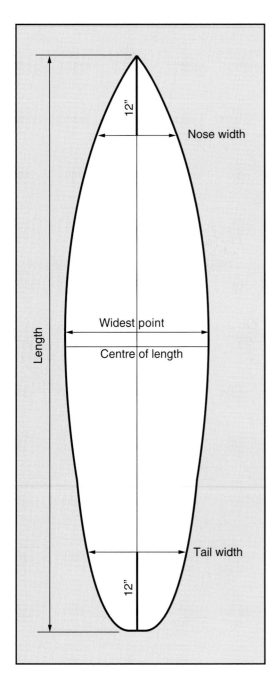

This chapter looks very briefly at surfboard design and basic repairs. If you want to follow the subject in more detail, there are books available covering board design and manufacture in much greater depth. The way a board is actually made is described later in the chapter – to start off we will look at the different features of a modern surfboard and what their functions are.

Template/Planshape

This is the basic shape of the board.

Length

The length of the board from the nose to the tail

Width

The widest part of the board. On modern shortboards this will usually vary between 19in/48cm and 21in/53cm, and its location on individual boards will vary from about 8in/20cm in front of the centre of the board to about 2in/5cm behind.

Nose width

This is the width of the board measured 12in/30.5cm from the tip of the nose.

Tail width

This is the width of the board measured 12in/30.5cm from the tail.

TAIL DESIGN

Tail designs come and go, but those below have all been seen on boards in the last few years, and those that are not so common these days will no doubt surface again in the future.

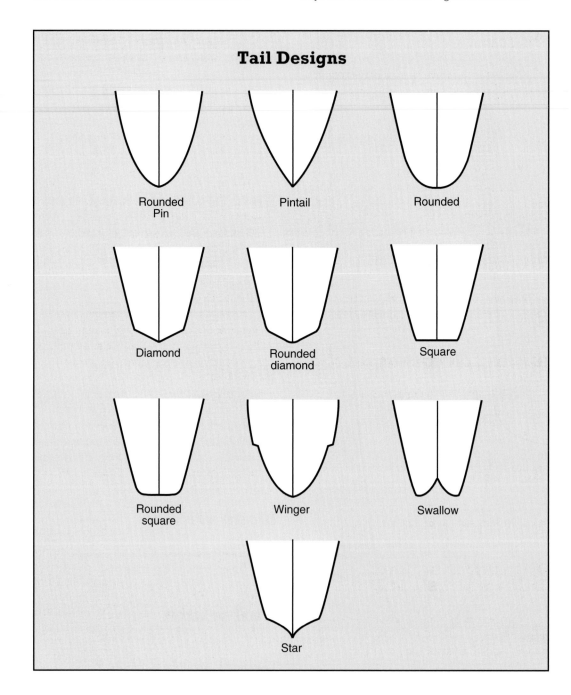

Tail Designs

Rounded Pin

Pintail

Rounded

Diamond

Rounded diamond

Square

Rounded square

Winger

Swallow

Star

Rounded pin

Probably the most common tail shape, and suitable for most types of surfing - it gives smooth turns and holds in well.

Pintail

This is the big wave version of the rounded pin, designed to hold in well in big surf.

Round tail

Another variation on the pintail, a rounded tail board is good in smaller surf due to its extra surface area which allows it to pick up the wave more easily.

Diamond tail

The sharper corners of the diamond tail result in a sharper turn than from a pintail.

Rounded diamond tail

Very similar to a round tail in both appearance and performance.

Square tail

The sharp edges of the square tail result in a very responsive board that turns easily.

Rounded square tail/squash tail

Very similar in appearance, both have a similar but somewhat more subdued performance than the square tail.

A shark can swallow anything half its size in one gulp. Only surf near small sharks.

Wingers

Wingers can feature in most board designs, and are usually situated between 3in/8cm and 12in/30cm from the tail. They combine the ability to hold in on a wave (from the narrow 'tail' behind the winger) with the looseness of a wider tail (in front of the wings). There may be from one to three pairs of wings on a board.

Swallow tail

A swallow tail combines the holding-in ability of a pintail (in effect it is two small pintails side-by-side) with the responsiveness of a square tail which results from the extra tail surface area.

Star tail

A combination of square/diamond tail and pintail, once again allowing the board to hold in well and be responsive in the turn.

Sharks have no sense of pain - in a feeding frenzy they will eat their own bodies.

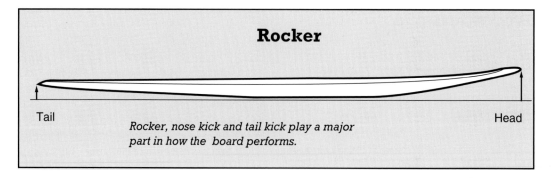

Rocker

Rocker, nose kick and tail kick play a major part in how the board performs.

Tail   Head

DESIGN ESSENTIALS

Rocker

Rocker is the bottom curve of a board which is most easily viewed side-on. A very curved rocker results in a board that turns tightly, but is harder to paddle, more difficult to catch waves on and is slower on the wave. Conversely, a flatter rocker gives a board that is more difficult to turn and more likely to pearl, but which will be easier to paddle, will catch waves more easily and is faster on the wave

Nose kick

This is the upward curve of the bottom of the board in the front third, caused by the rocker. This is important because a lack of nose kick can cause the board to pearl, while too much can lead to its pushing water ahead of it, giving a slow ride.

Tail kick

This is the curve of the rocker at the tail of the board. The more pronounced it is the tighter the board can turn.

Rail

The rail is the edge of the board. Hard rails have a sharper edge and cut through the water more, thus giving a more manoeuvrable board. Soft rails do not cut through the water so readily and give a smoother ride. They are more effective at holding into the wave (hard rails may break away from the water surface), so smooth rails are better for bigger waves where you

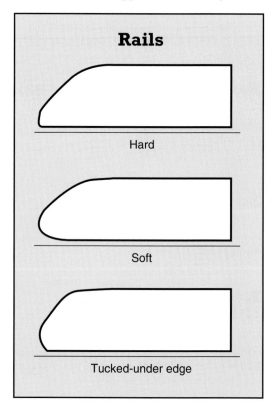

Rails

Hard

Soft

Tucked-under edge

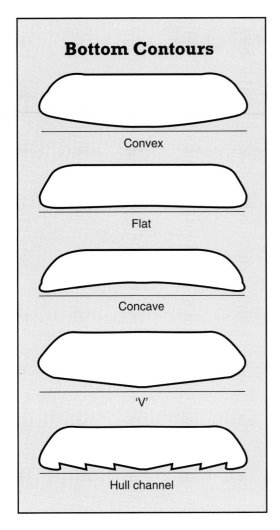

Bottom Contours

Convex

Flat

Concave

'V'

Hull channel

2. Flat is a responsive, loose shape, especially in small or 'gutless' waves. However in bigger waves flat bottoms have a tendency to plane a lot, making them prone to 'spinning out' (the tail slides away) in hard turns and more difficult to turn generally.

3. Concave is good at high speeds, as it contains the water flow down the length of the board and 'squeezes' it out at the tail, increasing the effectiveness of the fins.

4. 'V' bottom boards are often combined with convex bottoms, with the 'V' on the back third and the convex on the front two-thirds. This makes the tail responsive at high speeds, allowing the board to be turned more easily.

5. Channels direct water flow down the length of the board as they are incorporated at a concave angle. As with a concave bottom this 'squeezes' water out past the tail, but without compressing it in the way a concave bottom does, as the channels (there are usually between 4 and 8) run parallel to each other. This allows for easier turning.

☆ *Listen to the experts and take advice on what kind of board you need – only the very experienced can confidently dictate how much rocker or which tail shape suits them best.*

☆ *If you are buying a custom board, ask if you can see the shaper at work. It will give a valuable insight on how the different board shapes are made.*

need the board to hold in at speed. A tucked-under edge on the rail gives a combination of the qualities of hard and soft rails. Most modern boards will vary in rail hardness/softness along the length of the board.

Bottom contours

1. Convex is the least efficient bottom design – it parts the water like a plough which prevents the rails from slicing in effectively. However, it can be more effective when combined with other bottom designs.

8 Care & Repair

Surfing equipment does not come particularly cheap, so it's worth looking after. In particular, custom surfboards can be extremely fragile and won't last long without care and attention. Indeed, it is one of the unwritten laws of surfing that a new board collects 'dings' (small impact damage) quicker than a dog collects fleas.

CUSTOM CONSTRUCTION

When you look at how a board is made you will understand why it is so fragile if mishandled, yet at the same time can easily withstand the most intense stresses on a wave. The core of the board is a **blank** made from soft polyurethane foam. A **stringer**, which is a thin strip of balsa, runs down the centre of the blank to give strength and rigidity. The blank can easily be worked to the required shape by a shaper, although doing the job well requires skill and experience.

Once the blank has been shaped, it will be airbrushed to the customer's decorative requirements before the glassing takes place. This involves laminating the blank with fibreglass cloth and resin to give a hard outer surface. At this stage the fins are also fitted. A second coat of filler resin is applied before the board is sanded with an electric sander, followed by a filler coat and finishing with wet and dry paper and a polish.

DING DAMAGE

The glass laminate of a custom board is essentially a lightweight outer skin which has only a relatively low resistance to knocks and is easily penetrated. It could be made more ding resistant by using more resin, but that would increase the weight of the board considerably; alternatively the board builder could use a material such as carbon, but that would add considerable cost for no real gain.

If a standard custom board falls onto a hard surface, collides with another board, or is ridden into rocks, you will have a ding in your board and a repair on your hands. This needs to be done as soon as possible, or at the very least the hole should be sealed to prevent water getting into the foam. If water is allowed to get in, it can discolour the board or delaminate it which lifts the fibreglass away from the foam. Never delay – use duct tape to cover a ding, or in an emergency board wax can be pushed into a hole to seal it. You must get all the wax out again before you repair the hole.

However well you look after your board it is inevitable that it will collect a ding or two, but there are a few ways of reducing ding probability:

1. Never leave the board standing up against a wall or fence. It can easily fall if caught by the wind.
2. Do not wax-up on a hard surface – this can crack the glass, and any hard projections such as pebbles may hole the board. It also puts strain on the fins.
3. Get as good a quality board bag as you can afford. Alternatively an old sleeping bag will do.
4. When you strap the board to the roof of your car or van, don't overdo it – you could put a pressure ding in the rails if you tighten the straps too much, especially if they are narrow.

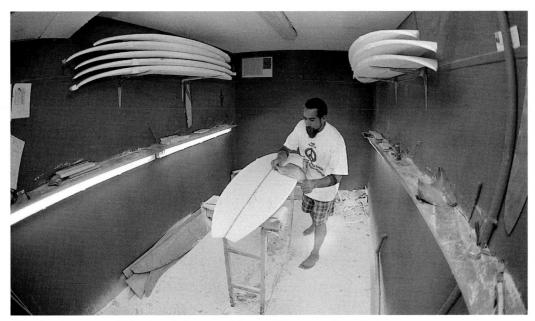

The shaping room of Maurice Cole, one of the world's top surfboard shapers.

(However, do take care that the board is secure and will not come undone at speed as you head for the beach.) You should also pad your roofrack with pipe insulation (or suchlike) to give a nice soft ride.

Ding repair

Small cracks and dents on the board may not always need repairing - it is only if water is getting into the foam that you need to do an immediate repair job. This is how you go about repairing a small ding:

1. Ensure there is no water in the ding - leave the board in the sun, ding-side down so it can drain, or use a hair dryer if you're in a rush. (Dings always happen with a good swell when you are rushing to get to it!)

2. Using a sharp knife, cut out any damaged foam or fibreglass and roughen the area to be bonded with coarse sandpaper.

3. Small dings can be repaired with chopped-up strands of fibreglass or small patches of fibreglass. Larger ones will require you to shape a piece of foam to match the hole you have cut. Make sure this is a tight fit. Then shape the dinged areas into a slight depression – this ensures the fibreglass that will go on top can lie flush with the board's surface.

4. Cut a strip of fibreglass to match the repair area, but overlapping slightly.

5. Mix the resin and catalyst. Repair kits will tell you what proportions to use, but the warmer the air temperature the less catalyst you need. Then

Time for a repair job! Time and patience plus a clean and clinical approach are needed to get it done correctly, but sometimes a board is beyond repair.

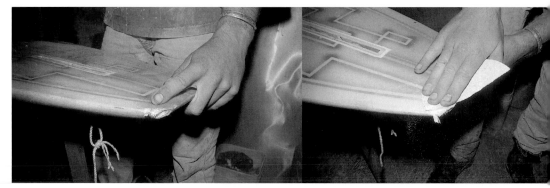

The plan is to 'repair' this ding.   *Sand down the damaged area.*

Mix resin and catalyst, following the instructions.   *Pour on the mix, leaving it slightly proud as*

brush the resin into the fibreglass over the foam, working it well in.

6. Build up this area with layers of resin-saturated fibreglass until it is slightly proud of the rest of the board. Alternatively you can pour resin on its own into the depression until it is level or slightly proud of the board – use masking tape to stop the resin draining away Before the resin has set, level out the glass and resin in the depression.

7. When the resin becomes rubbery, apply a final sanding coat. Once the whole lot has set sand it down, finishing off with wet-and-dry paper for a smooth finish, and a touch of T-cut for a final polish. Do not get too enthusiastic at the sanding stage or you could go through the glass to the foam.

Major dings and fin replacement can be done at

home, but they require more experience of board repair, and at first are probably best left to your local surf shop. If you do your own repairs, it is well worth wearing gloves and a mask, especially in a confined space becaude some of the materials involved are highly toxic. Always use clean implements. And one final tip – the gunk that is left on your hands at the end of all this (assuming you have failed to use gloves!) can be shifted with biological washing powder or washing-up liquid mixed with sugar.

WETSUIT MAINTENANCE

Wetsuits – especially winter steamers - can be a pain to get on and a real pain to take off. It may be tempting to rip off a suit as fast as

t a patch of fibreglass which slightly overlaps the repair area.

Mark off the repair area.

t hard, sand down but not through to the foam.

Finally rub with wet-and-dry followed by T-cut.

possible and throw it in a corner until it's needed again, but it won't last long with that kind of treatment. When you consider that for many surfers a wetsuit is by far the most expensive item of clothing that they own, it is something that deserves to be looked after.

When putting your suit on do it gradually, rolling and sliding it over your arms and legs rather than wrenching and tugging, which strains the seams. Fasten the zip carefully too – if it snags pull it down and clear the obstacle rather than yanking on it until something gives. If you are having problems with a back zip, ask someone to pull it up for you.

When removing your wetsuit roll it down over your arms, body and legs so that it's inside out. Then ease it over your wrists and ankles. If

you live in a cold climate you will soon learn to do this in record time.

After use always rinse it out with fresh water. This will help to stop the neoprene from rotting, drying and cracking, and will keep the zip in good order and prevent it jamming with salt. You could even give your suit a very gentle wash in a washing machine once in a while.

If you're on the beach in a thunderstorm, the safest place to be is behind a sand dune.

If you find tears or split seams, get them repaired as soon as possible – the bigger the damage gets the harder it will be to repair and the less effective it is likely to be. This may involve sending the suit back to the manufacturer. If the damage is not caused by your own misuse, remember that all good wetsuits should have at least a 12 month guarantee.

You may be able to repair smaller holes yourself using neoprene glue. It is also possible to repair conventional seams using a needle and thread, but if you have a wetsuit with sealed or 'blind stitched' seams the repair will need a special machine and must be done by an expert or the manufacturer.

CARE ON SURFARI

Once you decide to travel abroad with your stick, you need to pack it properly to make sure it arrives in one piece. Airline baggage handlers may claim to be a much-maligned breed when it comes to respecting other people's property, but with surfboards - well, that reputation had to come from somewhere!

Searching for surf in the Canaries. Great waves, but the rocky coastline is just waiting to ding your board and rip your wetsuit – if the baggage handlers haven't got there first.

When I travel I wrap every available soft item I can around my board before putting it into the board bag – wetsuit (making sure the zip is not in contact with the board), clothes, towel and anything else. It is also well worth taping bubble wrap around the rails, nose and tail of the board. The fins can be protected with a large block of polystyrene – cut holes for the fins and place it over the top. Alternatively there are patent fin protectors on the market.

All this is no guarantee that your pride and joy will emerge from its bag in the same condition that it went in, so also take a repair kit with you – and get good travel insurance that expressly covers damage to your board.

 **SURF TIPS**

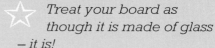

☆ *Wear a mask when repairing your board unless you are doing it in a very well ventilated area – like your garden.*

☆ *Treat your board as though it is made of glass – it is!*

☆ *Keep a repair kit to hand and learn to use it – you are bound to need it one day.*

☆ *Never rip and pull at your wetsuit to get it on or off.*

☆ *Pack your board with real care if you travel by air.*

9 Green Seas

Surfers are often the first to realise when something is wrong with our oceans, spending more time than most immersed in them. In recent years a number of environmental organisations have been formed by surfers throughout the world to campaign for cleaner oceans. One of the most dynamic of these has been the British group *Surfers Against Sewage*. Their General Secretary Chris Hines describes below what SAS is all about and how you too can become a member.

"Surfers Against Sewage was formed in May 1990 by a group of surfers who were fed up with becoming ill from sewage-polluted seawater. Tampons, condoms, human faeces and everything else we flush down our loos ends up in the sea and on the beaches. In the region of 300 million gallons of sewage is pumped into our ocean every day, despite there being alternative safer and cheaper methods of disposal.

SAS realised it was not just surfers who are at risk from this pollution, but everyone who uses the sea and beaches. Children, adults, locals, tourists, canoeists, windsurfers and even knee-deep paddlers all risk their good health every time they go to the beach. Something had to be done.

After the first public meeting word of the campaign spread thick and fast, firstly through the surfing community then branching out to interest non-surfers and non-coastal residents. SAS have always stressed that, despite the name, you do not have to know a thing about surfing to become a member. As a result of much successful publicity, an attention-grabbing name and a worthwhile cause, membership has spread nationally and soon rolled into the thousands.

Now SAS are one of the most successful pressure groups in the country, and have earned a reputation as THE authority in the sewage debate, although some of the profiteering fat cats might disagree. SAS's high-profile campaigning involves very visual demonstrations using the likes of huge inflatable faeces and a panty-liner surfboard. It also involves campaigning at very high levels. SAS have visited the House of Commons, the European Parliament, the House of Lords, the European Commission and the Monopolies and Mergers Commission in their quest to clean up the seas.

SAS try and involve members in active campaigning as much as possible. A quarterly newsletter, 'Pipeline News', is circulated to all SAS members as well as hundreds of media contacts across the country. This reports on SAS's recent movements and forewarns members of any demonstrations, surveys and fund raising events they might wish to be involved in.

The campaign is funded mainly through the sale of SAS merchandise and membership subscriptions. The more people who join, the more weight is added to the argument. So, if you are disgusted by the state of our oceans and the negligent attitude towards protecting the health of beach users please join SAS today – and maybe we can eventually return our coastlines to the safe playgrounds they should be!"

**Chris Hines, SAS, St. Agnes, Cornwall
Spring 1996**

Being safe in the knowledge that the sea is clean should be a fundamental right for all beach users, whether they are children paddling in the shallows or surfers out in the waves.

The following organisations are actively doing something to clean up our oceans – join one of them!

UK
Surfers Against Sewage
The Old Counthouse Warehouse,
Wheal Kitty, St Agnes, Cornwall TR5 0RE.

USA
The Surfrider Foundation
122 South El Camino Real, No 67,
San Clemente, CA 92672.

EUROPE
Surfrider Europe
Villa Sion, 79 Bis Rue d'Espagne,
64200 Biarritz, France.

AUSTRALIA
Surfrider Australia
PO Box 444, Mermaid Beach,
Queensland 4128.

JAPAN
Surfrider Japan
c/o Patagonia Japan, 1-13-12 Komachi,
Kamakura-Shi 248, Japan.

BRAZIL
Surfrider Brazil
Fundacao Solon 1069, Sao Paulo,
SP 01127-010, Brazil.

Two litres of engine oil will contaminate about $^1/_4$ million gallons of sea water.

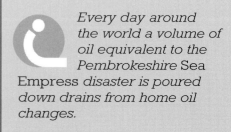

Every day around the world a volume of oil equivalent to the Pembrokeshire Sea Empress disaster is poured down drains from home oil changes.

10 Surfing Associations

The following organisations can advise you about surfing in their respective countries, supplying information that ranges from your nearest surf school to the next competition:

UK
British Surfing Association,
Champions Yard, Penzance, Cornwall,
England TR18 2SS.

Australia
Australian Surfriders Association,
PO Box 230, Torquay, Victoria,
Australia 3228.

Canada
Canadian Surf Association,
#1809-5599 Fenwick St, Halifax,
Nova Scotia, Canada B2H 1R2.

France
Federation Francaise de Surf,
BP 28 Plage Nord 40150,
Hossegor, France.

Hawaii
Hawaiian Surfing Federation,
Po Box 1707, Pearl City, Hawaii 96782.

Ireland
Irish Surfing Association,
Areelan Dale, Rossnowlagh,
Co. Donegal, Ireland.

New Zealand
New Zealand Surfing Association,
PO Box 12, Beachlands,
Auckland, New Zealand.

Portugal
Federacao Portuguesa de Surf,
Rua de San Pedro #42,
30-Esq Viana do Castello, Portugal.

South Africa
United Surfing Council of South Africa,
PO Box 127, Rondenbosch, 7700,
South Africa.

11   SurfSpeak

Surfing has a language of its own which sadder members of society, the media in particular, regularly dip into to add a touch of glamour to their dull lives. Here is a glossary to help beginners distinguish the real thing from the *wannabe*.

aerial: an advanced manoeuvre that involves taking off from the lip of the wave, travelling some distance through the air, then (in theory) landing back on the face of the wave and continuing the ride.

ASP: Association of Surfing Professionals - responsible for organising the annual world professional surfing circuit leading to the crowning of the world champion.

axed: hit by the lip of the wave, leading to a wipeout.

backhand: surfing with your back to the wave.

bank: sandbank on which waves break.

barrel: see *tube*

beach break: surf breaking on a sandy beach.

blank: block of foam from which a custom surfboard is made.

blown out: term for choppy surf resulting from onshore winds.

bombora: a deep water, offshore reef break.

boogie board: a soft foam board ridden on the belly by those who can't or won't stand up. Also known as a 'sponge' or 'esky lid'.

bottom turn: a turn at the bottom of the wave face.

carving: powerful, high-energy surfing.

Carving the face of a small beach break – there's still nothing like it.

catalyst: ingredient used to make resin harden (also known as hardener). Very toxic.

channel: deep water gap between sandbanks or reefs, or design feature on underside of a surfboard.

clean: glassy, peeling waves and/or good surf conditions.

clean-up: a large set that catches everybody 'inside'.

Nowhere to run – a close-out wave brings this ride to an end.

close-out: a wave that breaks along its entire length simultaneously – no good for surfing.

concave: bottom design on a surfboard aimed to give extra lift.

cutback: a turn on the face of the wave that takes you back towards the white water.

deck: upper surface of a board.

delamination: when the fibreglass 'skin' of a board becomes separated from the foam.

ding: a dent or hole in the surfboard – get it fixed!

drop (to take the drop): to take off on a breaking wave and ride down the (usually steep) face to the bottom.

drop in: when one surfer takes off on a wave already being ridden by another surfer nearer the peak – very bad style!

duck dive: method of getting through a breaking or broken wave while paddling out.

eskimo roll: another method for getting through a wave, mostly used with mini-mals and longboards.

face: the unbroken surface of a wave (also known as the green water).

Floating on a carpet of foam and air...

forehand: surfing with your face to the wave.

floater: a manoeuvre that involves launching the board off the lip of the wave onto a section of broken or breaking wave in front, unweighting, and free-falling down the face with the breaking white water.

glassy: smooth seas resulting from calm wind conditions – provides excellent surf when combined with a swell.

gnarly: heavy, difficult waves, usually quite big.

goofy foot: a surfer who surfs with his or her right foot forward on the board.

Goofy-foot action on a fast right-hand beach break.

grommet: young and precocious surfer.

groundswell: a clean swell with evenly-spaced lines, usually from a distant storm.

gun: a big wave board - long and narrow in shape.

hang five: to ride with five toes curled over the nose of the board – more common on longboards.

hang ten: to ride with all ten toes over the nose – a stylish and difficult longboard manoeuvre.

hollow: a cylindrical wave – common with powerful swells and offshore winds.

impact zone: the point at which a swell is breaking most heavily and most frequently.

indicator: an offshore deep-water reef or bank. Only a big swell or a big set will break on this, so it acts as a good indicator of something big approaching.

inside: shoreward of a breaking wave or set (as in 'caught inside'), or an expression for life in the tube. The inside rail is the one nearest the wave face.

kick-out: to make a controlled exit from a wave by riding up the face and over the top.

Dolphins sleep with one eye open - sharks never sleep.

Hitting the lip.

leash: urethane cord which attaches the board to the surfer by means of a velcro strap.

left-hander (left): a wave that breaks from left to right when viewed from shore.

line-up: the point where you sit, just outside the break, and wait to catch a wave.

lined-up: term to describe an even, well developed swell.

lip: the crest of a wave, which may 'throw out' to create a tube.

Malibu board: another term for a longboard - usually between 8ft 6in/2.60m and 10ft 6in/3.20m in length. Named after the beach in Southern California.

Taking the drop on a clean left-hander.

Offshore conditions, making the wave hollow enough for the surfer to get way back in the tube.

maxed-out: a break is said to be 'maxed out' when the swell is so big it will no longer break cleanly, but will close out or 'section'.

natural or natural foot: a surfer who surfs with his left foot forward, which is the natural stance.

nose: the front of the board.

Surfing animals include – dolphins, porpoises, seals, sea otters, dogs and parrots (on boards).

nose-riding: technique used by longboarders who attempt to ride as close to the nose of the board as possible.

off the lip/lip bash: manoeuvre whereby the board hits the breaking lip of the wave before continuing along the wave.

offshore: when the wind is blowing from the land out to sea and holding up the face of the wave – will usually produce ideal surfing conditions, especially when the wind is reasonably light.

onshore: when the wind is blowing from the sea onto the land – this messes up the wave face and produces poor surfing conditions.

outside, or out the back: the area beyond the impact zone. The outside rail is the edge furthest from the wave face.

over the falls: to fall down the face of the wave inside the falling lip.

peak: the point at which a wave breaks first, from which it ideally peels in one or both directions.

peel: a wave is said to peel when it breaks away evenly and cleanly from the peak.

pearl: this is when the nose of the board buries itself underwater and the surfer usually shoots over the front. Most common on take-offs.

pocket: the steepest and most powerful part of the wave, just ahead and under the breaking lip.

point break: a break where the waves are refracted around a headland or point and then peel along the inside of the point.

pop-out: a machine moulded surfboard, ideal for beginners.

prone-out: dropping from your feet to your belly to ride the board into the beach.

pumping: term used to describe a good, powerful swell.

pumping the board: a means of increasing speed across the face of a wave.

quiver: a selection of surfboards for differing conditions.

rail: the side or edge of a board.

Enjoying the action at La Santa Point on Lanzarote – one of Europe's best point breaks.

Taking the tube...

reef break: waves breaking over a projection rising from the sea bed – usually a coral reef or rock shelf.

re-entry: manoeuvre which involves surfing up into the lip of a breaking wave, then coming back down with it.

resin: chemical used in a two-part mixture with catalyst to convert fibreglass into a hard outer skin.

right-hander (right): a wave that breaks from right to left when viewed from the shore.

rip: a channel of water running out to sea.

rocker: the curve in a surfboard when viewed side-on.

sandbank: an elevation in the level of the sea floor on a beach, causing waves to break over it.

set: a group of waves.

shore break: a wave that breaks close in to the beach.

shoulder: the unbroken face of a wave ahead of the white water.

soup: the white water of a broken wave.

spin-out: when the fins of the board break loose from the water surface.

spring suit: wetsuit with short arms and short legs.

stall: a manoeuvre where the board is slowed, or 'stalled', to allow the curl to catch up with the rider.

steamer: a full wetsuit with long arms and long legs.

stringer: the thin piece of wood running down the centre of a custom board.

sucky: a hollow, often heavy wave.

switch-foot: a surfer who can surf with either foot forward.

tail: the rear end of the board, which can have a number of different shapes.

take-off: the start of a ride.

three-sixty: spinning the board through 360 degrees on the face of the wave.

thruster: a three-finned surfboard.

trimming: adjusting weight and position on the board so that the board retains maximum speed.

tube: the inside of a hollow wave.

vee: convex shape on the bottom of a board.

windswell: a weak swell generated by localised winds.

wipeout: do you really need to know!

There are around 30 shark attacks world-wide per year.

Some reviews of Wayne Alderson's ealier book, Surf UK.

The first thing you should know about this book is that it is the most comprehensive guide to Britain's surfing beaches ever published.

This is the book you will keep in the glove box of your car for whenever you surf somewhere new. This is the British beach bum's bible.

Wavelength
April 1995

Excellent.. Wayne Alderson has been everywhere and done everything.

Surf Magazine
June 1995

Full details on the surf at 400 breaks around Britain.

Guardian
August 1995

If you have enjoyed reading this book, you should also check out other great surfing publications by Fernhurst Books...

Surf UK (second edition)

A guide to the UK's surf beaches by Wayne Alderson

This is a comprehensive, 160 page guide to nearly 400 British surfing beaches with maps, diagrams and photos of the local action. Full details are given on the breaks, access, facilities, accommodation and surf shops in the area. There's also an eight page colour guide to Britain's surf beaches.

The History of Surfing

2nd edition of the surfing 'Classic' by Nat Young

A magnificent, inspiring, full-colour, 200 page, big format history of this glorious sport.

SURF SHOPS

ABERSOCH WATERSPORTS
The Bridge
Hells Mouth
Abersoch
Gwynedd LL53 7DY

Tel/Surfline: 01758 712483
Fax: 01758 713818

ANNAPURNA
Surfing and Climbing Shop
Haverfordwest
Pembrokeshire

Tel: 01437 767517

ANN'S COTTAGE SURF SHOP
Polzeath
Wadebridge
Cornwall

Tel: 01208 863317
Fax: 01208 862080

ATLANTIC AQUASPORTS
Albert Street
Penzance
Cornwall TR18 2LR

Tel: 01736 65757
Fax: 01736 51626

ATTITUDE SURF
On the Beach
Tramore
Co. Waterford
Ireland

Surf Report on: 051 390031
Mobile: 088 566662
Fax: 051 381423

BATHSHEBA SURF
19 St. Pirans Road
Perranporth
Cornwall TR6 0BH

Tel/Fax: 01872 573748

BEACH SHOP 'N' SURF
Seafront
Lower Tregea Hill
Portreath
Cornwall TR16 4NN

Tel: 01209 842920

BOURNEMOUTH SURFING
127 Bellevue Road
Southbourne
Bournemouth
Dorset BH6 3DJ

Tel: 01202 433544
Fax/Surfcheck: 01202 434344

CAYTON BAY SURF SHOP
Killerby Park
Killerby Cliff
Cayton Bay
Scarborough
North Yorkshire YO11 3NR

Tel: 01723 582495

CROYDE BAY SURF HIRE
Croyde Bay
North Devon EX33 1NP

Tel/Fax: 01271 890453

FISTRAL SURF CO. (2 shops)
19 Cliff Road
Newquay
Cornwall TR7 1SG

Tel/Fax: 01637 850378

1 Beacon Road
Newquay
Cornwall TR7 1HH

Tel: 01637 876169

FREERIDE SURF
32 Haven Road
Canford Cliffs
Poole
Dorset BH13 7LP

Tel: 01202 708555
Fax: 01202 709432

HARBOUR SPORTS (2 Shops)
The Harbour
Paignton
Devon TQ4 6DT

Tel: 01803 550180
Fax: 01803 558084

The Barbican
Plymouth
Devon PL1 2JL

Tel: 01752 660604
Fax: 01752 250400

HAVEN SPORTS
Marine Road
Broadhaven
Haverfordwest
Pembrokeshire
Dyfed SA62 3JR

Tel/Fax: 01437 781354

LEISURE LAKES (3 Shops)
Mere Brow
Tarleton
Preston
Lancashire PR4 6JX

Tel: 01772 814990
Fax: 01772 815896

110 Wash Lane
Bury
Lancashire BL9 7DJ

Tel: 0161 797 5625
Fax: 0161 797 4332

4 Station Road
Retail Park
Vicar Lane
Daventry
Northants NN11 5AA

Tel: 01327 310400
Fax: 01327 311026

MACH ENTERPRISES (2 Shops)
4-8 Lady Lawson Street
Edinburgh
Scotland EH3 9DS

Tel: 0131 229 5887
Fax: 0131 228 1707

1146 Argyll Street
Glasgow
Scotland G3 1AA

Tel: 0141 334 5559
Fax: 0141 357 4476

MANCHESTER WATERSPORTS
5 Bentinck Street
Chester Road
Manchester M15 4LN

Tel: 0161 839 8988
Fax: 0161 834 3116

NEWGALE FILLING STATION
Newgale
Haverfordwest
Pembrokeshire

Tel: 01437 721398
Surf Report: 01437 720698

OCEAN SPORTS
The Surf Shop
368 Kingsway
Hove
Sussex BN3 4QT

Tel: 01273 412241
Fax: 01273 412246

PIRAN SURFSHOP
38 St. Pirans Road
Perranporth
Cornwall TR6 0BJ

Tel: 01872 573242
Fax: 01872 573244

P.J.'s SURF SHOP
Western House
Llangennith
West Glamorgan

Tel/Fax: 01792 3866669

POLKERRIS WINDSURFING
Lifeboat Cafe
Polkerris By Fowey
Cornwall PL28 2TL

Tel/Fax: 01726 815142

RIVER DEEP MOUNTAIN HIGH
Middle Street
Galway
Ireland

Tel/Fax: 00353 91563938

SHORE WATERSPORTS (2
20 Shore Road
East Wittering
Chichester
West Sussex PO20 8L

Tel: 01243 672315
Fax: 01243 673759

North Ney Marina
Hayling Island
Hants PO11 0NH

Tel: 01705 467334
Fax: 01705 468107

Surfline: 0839 337760
39p per minute cheap / 49p ot

SURFERS AGAINST SEW
The Old Counthouse
Warehouse
Wheal Kitty
St. Agnes
Truro
Cornwall TR5 0RE

Tel: 01872 552505
Fax: 01872 552615

THE BAY SURF SHOP
Barton Road
Woolacombe
Devon EX34 7BA

Tel/Fax: 01271 870961

THE SURF SHACK (2 Sho
Market Road
Rye
East Sussex TN31 3J.

Tel: 01797 225746

13 Market Buildings
Maidstone
Kent ME14 1HP

Tel: 01622 661997

WEST COAST SURF SHO
Lon Pen Cei
Abersoch
Pwllheli
Gwynedd LL53 7AP

Surf Check and gene
enquiries:
0175871 3067

WET & WILD ADVENTURE SI
619 Anlaby Road
Hull
Humberside HU3 6SL

Tel: 01482 354076
Fax: 01482 354972

ZUMA JAYS
Bellevue Lane
Bude
Cornwall EX23 8BR

Tel/Fax: 01288 354956